cook's library
Chicken

cook's library
Chicken

p

This is a Parragon Publishing Book
This edition published in 2003

Parragon Publishing
Queen Street House
4 Queen Street
Bath BA1 1HE, UK

ISBN: 0-75259-950-x

Printed in China

NOTE

This book uses metric and imperial measurements. Follow the same
units of measurement throughout; do not mix metric and imperial.
All spoon measurements are level: teaspoons are assumed to be 5 ml,
and tablespoons are assumed to be 15 ml. Unless otherwise stated,
milk is assumed to be full fat, eggs and individual vegetables, such as
potatoes are medium, and pepper is freshly ground black pepper.

The times given for each recipe are an approximate guide only because the
preparation times may differ according to the techniques used by different
people and the cooking times may vary as a result of the type of oven used.
The preparation times include chilling and marinating times, where appropriate.

Recipes using raw or very lightly cooked eggs should be
avoided by infants, the elderly, pregnant women, convalescents,
and anyone suffering from an illness.

Contents

Introduction

Chicken has become justly popular around the world and plays an important part in the modern diet, being reasonably priced and nutritionally sound. A versatile meat, it lends itself to an enormous range of cooking methods and cuisines. Its unassertive flavor means that it is equally suited to both sweet and savory flavors.

Since it has a low fat content, especially without the skin, it is an ideal meat for low cholesterol and calorie-controlled diets. As well as being an excellent source of protein, chicken contains valuable minerals, such as potassium and phosphorus, and some of the B vitamins.

The recipes included in this book come from many countries and cultures. Grouped into sections, they reflect the wonderful versatility of chicken. There are recipes for warming, wholesome chicken soups, simple snacks and appetizers, slow-cooked casseroles, tempting roast meals, low-fat stir-fries, mouthwatering grills and barbecues, and fragrant spicy dishes.

Trying out new recipes, even with familiar ingredients, is fun and a great way to encourage healthier eating. For great results every time, follow the information on the next pages explaining the different cooking techniques, as well as the advice on storing, handling, and preparing raw chicken. Take advantage, too, of the section of recipes for basic stocks and other essential ingredients needed for many of the main dishes.

Cooking techniques

Roasting

To prepare a chicken for roasting, remove any fat from the body cavity. Rinse the bird inside and out with water, then pat dry with paper towels. Season the cavity generously with salt and pepper and add stuffing, herbs, or lemon, if wished. Spread the breast of the chicken with softened butter or oil. Set on a rack in a roasting pan or shallow baking pan. Roast the bird, basting two or three times with the pan juices during cooking. If the chicken browns too quickly, cover it with foil. Use a meat thermometer or insert a skewer into the thickest part of the thigh to see if the meat is done. If the chicken is cooked, the juices will run clear with no trace of pink. Put the bird on a carving board and let rest for 15 minutes before serving. Make a sauce or gravy from the juices left in the pan.

Broiling

The intense heat of the broiler quickly seals the succulent flesh of the chicken beneath a crisp, golden exterior. Place the chicken 10–15 cm/4–6 inches away from a moderate heat source. If the chicken seems to be browning too quickly, reduce the heat slightly. If the chicken is broiled at too high a temperature too near to the heat, the outside will burn before the inside is cooked. If it is cooked for too long under a low heat, it will dry out. Divide the chicken into joints to ensure even cooking. Breast meat, if cooked in one piece, can be rather dry, so it is best to cut it into chunks for kebabs. Wings are the best cut for speedy broiling.

Frying

This method of cooking is suitable for small thighs, drumsticks, and joints. Dry the chicken pieces with paper towels so that they brown properly and to prevent spitting during cooking. The chicken can be coated in seasoned flour, egg, and bread crumbs, or a batter. Heat the oil or a mixture of oil and butter in a deep skillet. When the oil is very hot, add the chicken pieces, skin-side down. Cook until deep golden brown all over, turning the pieces frequently during cooking. Drain well on paper towels before serving.

Sautéing

Ideal for small pieces or small birds, such as baby chickens. Heat a little oil, or oil and butter in a heavy skillet. Fry the chicken over moderate heat until golden, turning frequently. Add bouillon or other liquid, bring to a boil, cover and reduce the heat. Cook the chicken gently until done.

Stir-frying

Perfect for skinless, boneless chicken pieces of equal size to ensure that the meat cooks evenly and stays succulent. Preheat a wok or pan then add a small amount of oil. When the oil starts to smoke, add the chicken and stir-fry with your chosen flavorings for 3–4 minutes, until cooked through. Cook other ingredients at the same time, or remove the cooked chicken from the pan while you stir-fry the remaining ingredients, returning the chicken to the pan once they are done.

Casseroling

A good method for cooking joints from larger, more mature chickens, although smaller chickens can also be cooked whole. The slow cooking produces tender meat with a good flavor. Brown the chicken in butter or oil or a mixture of both. Add some bouillon, wine, or a mixture, cover, and cook in the oven until the chicken is tender. Add a selection of lightly sautéed vegetables about halfway through the cooking time.

Braising

A method which requires little or no liquid. The chicken pieces or a small whole chicken and vegetables are cooked together slowly in a low oven. Heat some oil in an ovenproof, flameproof casserole and gently cook the chicken until golden. Remove the chicken and sauté a selection of vegetables until they are almost tender. Replace the chicken, cover tightly and cook very gently on the top of the stove or in a low oven until the chicken and vegetables are tender.

Poaching

A gentle cooking method that produces tender chicken and a bouillon that can be used to make a sauce to serve with the chicken. Put a whole chicken, bouquet garni, leek, carrot, and onion in a large flameproof casserole. Cover with water, season, and bring to a boil. Simmer for $1\frac{1}{2}$–2 hours, until the chicken is tender. Lift the chicken out, discard the bouquet garni, and use the bouillon to make a sauce. Blend the vegetables to thicken the bouillon and serve with the chicken.

Food Safety & Tips

When storing, handling, and preparing poultry, certain precautions must be observed to prevent the possibility of food poisoning. Chicken can become contaminated by salmonella bacteria, which can cause severe food poisoning.

- Check the sell-by date and best before date. After buying, take the chicken home quickly, preferably in a freezer bag or cool box.

- Put frozen birds immediately in the freezer.

- If storing in the refrigerator, remove the wrappings and store any giblets separately. Place the chicken in a shallow dish to catch any drips. Cover loosely with foil and store on the bottom shelf of the refrigerator for no more than 2–3 days, depending on the best before date. Avoid any contact between raw chicken and cooked food during storage and preparation. Wash your hands thoroughly after handling raw chicken.

- Prepare raw chicken on a chopping board that can be easily cleaned and bleached, such as a non-porous, plastic cutting board.

- Frozen birds should be defrosted before cooking. If time permits, defrost for about 36 hours in the refrigerator, or thaw for about 12 hours in a cool place. Bacteria breed in warm food at room temperature and when chicken is thawing. Cooking at high temperatures kills bacteria. There should be no ice crystals and the flesh should feel soft and flexible. Cook the chicken as soon as possible after thawing.

- Make sure that the chicken is cooked. Test if the chicken is done by using a meat thermometer—the thigh should reach at least 175°F when cooked. Otherwise, pierce the thickest part of a thigh with a skewer—the juices should run clear, not pink or red. Never partially cook chicken with the intention of completing the cooking later.

Basic Recipes

These recipes form the basis of several of the dishes contained in this book. Many of these basic recipes can be made in advance and stored in the refrigerator until required.

Fresh Chicken Bouillon

MAKES
7½ CUPS

2 lb 4 oz/1 kg chicken, skinned
2 celery stalks, chopped
1 onion, sliced
2 carrots, chopped
1 garlic clove
few sprigs of fresh parsley
9 cups water
salt and pepper

1 Place all the ingredients in a large saucepan. Bring to a boil.

2 Skim away surface scum using a large flat spoon. Reduce the heat to a gentle simmer, partially cover, and cook for 2 hours. Let cool.

3 Line a strainer with clean cheesecloth and place over a large pitcher or bowl. Pour the bouillon through the strainer. The cooked chicken can be used in another recipe. Discard the other solids. Cover the bouillon and chill.

4 Skim away any fat that forms on the top before using. Store, covered, in the refrigerator for up to 3 days, until required, or freeze the bouillon in small batches.

Fresh Vegetable Bouillon

MAKES
7½ CUPS

1 large onion, sliced
1 large carrot, diced
1 celery stalk, chopped
2 garlic cloves
1 dried bay leaf
few sprigs of fresh parsley
pinch of grated nutmeg
9 cups water
salt and pepper

1 Place the ingredients in a large saucepan and bring to a boil.

2 Skim away any surface scum using a large flat spoon. Reduce the heat to a gentle simmer, partially cover, and cook for 45 minutes. Let cool.

3 Line a strainer with clean cheesecloth and place over a large pitcher or bowl. Pour the bouillon through the strainer. Discard the solids.

4 Cover the bouillon and store in the refrigerator for up to 3 days, until required, or freeze in small batches for later use.

Cornstarch Paste

Mix 1 part cornstarch with about 1.5 parts of cold water. Stir until smooth. The paste can be used to thicken sauces.

Fresh Bouquet Garni

1 fresh or dried bay leaf
few sprigs of fresh parsley
few sprigs of fresh thyme

Tie the herbs together with a length of string or cotton.

Dried Bouquet Garni

1 dried bay leaf
good pinch of dried mixed herbs or any one herb
good pinch of dried parsley
8–10 black peppercorns
2–4 cloves
1 garlic clove (optional)

Put all the ingredients in a small square of cheesecloth and secure with string or cotton, leaving a long tail so it can be tied to the handle of the pan for easy removal.

Chinese Bouillon

MAKES
2¼ QUARTS

1 lb 10 oz /750 g chicken pieces, trimmed
  and chopped
1 lb 10 oz/750 g pork spare ribs, trimmed
  and chopped
3 quarts cold water
3–4 pieces fresh gingerroot, crushed
3–4 scallions, each tied into a knot
3–4 tbsp Chinese rice wine or dry sherry

1 Place the chicken and pork in a
  large pan with the water. Add the
  ginger and scallion knots.

2 Bring to a boil, and skim off the
  any scum with a large flat spoon.
  Reduce the heat and simmer,
  uncovered, for at least 2–3 hours.

3 Strain the bouillon, discarding
  the chicken, pork, ginger, and
  scallions. Add the wine and
  return to a boil. Reduce the heat
  and simmer for 2–3 minutes.
  Let cool.

4 Cover the bouillon and store in
  the refrigerator for up to 5 days,
  until required, or freeze in small
  batches for later use.

Fresh Beef Bouillon

MAKES
3 PINTS/7½ CUPS

about 2 lb 4 oz/1 kg bones from a cooked
  joint or raw chopped beef
2 onions, studded with 6 cloves, or sliced
  or chopped coarsely
2 carrots, sliced
1 leek, sliced
1–2 celery stalks, sliced
1 Bouquet Garni
about 2 quarts water

1 Use chopped marrow bones with
  a few strips of shin of beef if
  possible. Put in a roasting pan
  and cook in a preheated oven,
  450°F/230°C for 30–50 minutes,
  until browned.

2 Transfer to a large pan with the
  other ingredients. Bring to a boil
  and remove any scum from the
  surface with a large flat spoon.

3 Reduce the heat, cover, and
  simmer gently for 3–4 hours.
  Strain the bouillon and let cool.
  Remove any fat from the surface
  and chill. If stored for more than
  24 hours, the bouillon must be
  boiled every day, cooled quickly
  and chilled again.

4 The bouillon may be frozen for up
  to 2 months; place in a large
  plastic bag and seal, leaving at
  least 1-inch/2.5-cm of headspace
  to allow for expansion.

Fresh Fish Bouillon

MAKES
3 PINTS/7½ CUPS

2 lb 4 oz/1 kg white fish bones, heads,
  and scraps
1 large onion, chopped
2 carrots, chopped
2 celery stalks, chopped
½ tsp black peppercorns
½ tsp grated lemon zest
few sprigs of fresh parsley
9 cups water
salt and pepper

1 Rinse the fish trimmings in cold
  water and place in a large pan
  with the other ingredients.

2 Bring to a boil and skim off any
  scum from the surface with a
  large flat spoon.

3 Reduce the heat and simmer,
  partially covered, for 30 minutes.
  Let cool.

4 Line a strainer with clean
  cheesecloth and place over a
  large pitcher or bowl. Pour the
  bouillon through the strainer.
  Discard the solids.

5 Cover the bouillon and store in
  the refrigerator for up to 3 days
  until required, or freeze in small
  batches for later use.

How to Use This Book

Each recipe contains a wealth of useful information, including a breakdown of nutritional quantities, preparation and cooking times, and level of difficulty. All of this information is explained in detail below.

A full-color photograph of the finished dish.

The ingredients for each recipe are listed in the order that they are used.

The nutritional information provided for each recipe is per serving or per portion. Optional ingredients, variations, or serving suggestions have not been included in the calculations.

The method is clearly explained with step-by-step instructions that are easy to follow.

Cook's tips provide useful information regarding ingredients or cooking techniques.

⭐ The number of stars represents the difficulty of each recipe, ranging from very easy (1 star) to challenging (4 stars).

This amount of time represents the preparation of ingredients, including cooling, chilling, and soaking times.

🕐 This represents the cooking time.

Soups

Chicken soup has an established reputation of being comforting and good for us, and some cultures even think of it as a cure for all ills. It is certainly satisfying, full of flavor, and easy to digest. For the best results, use a good homemade chicken bouillon, although when time is at a premium, a good-quality bouillon cube can be used instead. Every cuisine in the world has its own favorite version of chicken soup and in this section you'll find a selection of recipes from as far afield as Italy, Scotland, Ireland, and China.

This refreshing soup with its tangy lemon flavor is perfect on a summer's day.

Lemon Chicken Soup

SERVES 4

4 tbsp butter
8 shallots, sliced thinly
2 carrots, sliced thinly
2 celery stalks, sliced thinly
9 oz/ 250 g skinless, boneless chicken breast, chopped finely
grated rind and juice of 3 lemons
5 cups chicken bouillon
²⁄₃ cup heavy cream
salt and pepper

to garnish
sprigs of fresh parsley
lemon slices

1 Melt the butter in a large pan, add the vegetables and chicken, and cook gently for 8 minutes.

2 Blanch the lemon rind in boiling water for 3 minutes.

3 Add the lemon rind and juice to the pan with the chicken bouillon, then bring slowly to a boil.

4 Reduce the heat and simmer for about 50 minutes. Let the soup cool, then transfer to a food processor and blend until smooth. Return the soup to the pan, reheat, season with salt and pepper to taste, and add the heavy cream. Do not boil at this stage or the soup will curdle.

5 Transfer the soup to a warm tureen or individual bowls. Serve, garnished with parsley and lemon slices.

NUTRITION
Calories *560*; Sugars *4 g*; Protein *19 g*;
Carbohydrate *41 g*; Fat *31 g*; Saturates *19 g*

 easy

15 mins

1 hr 15 mins

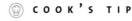 **COOK'S TIP**

For an alternative citrus flavor, use 3 oranges in place of the lemons. The recipe can also be adapted to make duck and orange soup.

Potatoes have been part of the Irish diet for centuries. This recipe is originally from the north of Ireland, in the beautiful area of Moira, County Down.

Irish Chicken Soup

1 Gently dry-fry the bacon and chicken in a large pan for 10 minutes.

2 Add the butter, potatoes, and onions and cook for 15 minutes, stirring all the time.

3 Add the bouillon and milk, then bring the soup to a boil. Reduce the heat and simmer for 45 minutes. Season with salt and pepper to taste.

4 Blend in the cream and simmer for 5 minutes. Stir in the parsley, transfer the soup to a warm tureen or individual bowls, and serve with soda bread.

SERVES 4

3 smoked, lean, rindless bacon slices, chopped
1 lb 2 oz/500g skinless, boneless chicken, chopped
2 tbsp butter
3 potatoes, chopped
3 onions, chopped
2¹/₂ cups giblet or chicken bouillon
2¹/₂ cups milk
²/₃ cup heavy cream
2 tbsp chopped fresh parsley
salt and pepper
soda bread, to serve

NUTRITION
Calories 97; Sugars 2 g; Protein 7 g; Carbohydrate 4 g; Fat 2 g; Saturates 3 g

moderate

10 mins

1 hr 20 mins

COOK'S TIP

Unlike most bread, soda bread is not made with yeast. Instead it uses baking soda as the rising agent. It can be made with all-purpose or whole-wheat flour.

This satisfying, filling soup can be served as a main course. You can add rice and bell peppers to make it even more hearty, as well as colorful.

Chicken *and* Leek Soup

SERVES 6

2 tbsp butter

12 oz/350g skinless, boneless chicken, cut into 1-inch/2.5-cm pieces

12 oz/350 g leeks, cut into 1-inch/ 2.5-cm pieces

5 cups chicken bouillon

1 bouquet garni

8 ready-to-eat pitted prunes, halved

cooked rice and diced bell peppers (optional)

salt and white pepper

1 Melt the butter in a large pan. Add the chicken and leeks, and cook for 8 minutes, stirring occasionally.

2 Add the chicken bouillon and bouquet garni to the pan. Season with salt and pepper to taste and bring the soup to a boil

3 Reduce the heat and simmer over a gentle heat for 45 minutes.

4 Add the prunes with some cooked rice and bell peppers, if using, and simmer for 20 minutes. Remove the bouquet garni and discard. Pour the soup into a warm tureen or individual bowls and serve.

NUTRITION

Calories *183*; Sugars *4 g*; Protein *21 g*; Carbohydrate *4 g*; Fat *9 g*; Saturates *5 g*

 very easy

5 mins

1 hr 15 mins

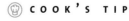 **COOK'S TIP**

If you have time, make the chicken bouillon yourself. Alternatively, you can buy good fresh bouillon from stores.

Quick to make, this hot and spicy soup is hearty and warming. If you like your food really fiery, add a chopped dried chili or a fresh chile with its seeds.

Thai-spiced Chicken Soup

1 Put the noodles in a shallow dish and soak in boiling water, according to the instructions on the package.

2 Heat the oil in a preheated wok or large, heavy-based pan. Add the chicken and cook for 5 minutes, stirring until lightly browned. Add the white part of the scallions, the garlic, and ginger and sauté for 2 minutes, stirring.

3 Add the bouillon, coconut milk, curry paste, peanut butter, and soy sauce. Season with salt and pepper to taste, then bring to a boil. Reduce the heat and simmer for 8 minutes, stirring occasionally. Add the red bell pepper, peas, and green scallion tops and cook for 2 minutes.

4 Add the drained noodles and heat through. Spoon into individual bowls and serve with a spoon and fork.

SERVES 4

1 sheet of dried egg noodles from a 9 oz/
    250 g pack
1 tbsp oil
4 skinless, boneless chicken thighs, diced
1 bunch scallions, sliced
2 garlic cloves, chopped
³/₄-inch/2-cm piece of fresh gingerroot,
    chopped finely
3³/₄ cups chicken bouillon
scant 1 cup coconut milk
3 tsp Thai red curry paste
3 tbsp peanut butter
2 tbsp light soy sauce
1 small red bell pepper, seeded and
    chopped
¹/₂ cup frozen peas
salt and pepper

NUTRITION
Calories *196*; Sugars *4 g*; Protein *16 g*;
Carbohydrate *8 g*; Fat *11 g*; Saturates *2 g*

   easy

10 mins

  25 mins

👨‍🍳 **COOK'S TIP**

If preferred, Thai green curry paste can be used instead of the red curry paste for a less fiery flavor.

This satisfying soup makes a good lunch or supper dish, and you can use any vegetables that you have at hand. Children will love the tiny pasta shapes.

Chicken *and* Pasta Broth

SERVES 6

2 tbsp sunflower oil
12 oz/350 g skinless, boneless chicken breasts, diced
1 onion, diced
1½ cups carrots, diced
9 oz/250 g cauliflower flowerets
3¾ cups chicken bouillon
2 tsp dried mixed herbs
4½ oz/125 g small pasta shapes
salt and pepper
Parmesan cheese (optional)
crusty bread, to serve

1 Heat the oil in a large pan and sauté the chicken and vegetables until they are lightly colored.

2 Stir in the bouillon and herbs. Bring to a boil and add the pasta shapes. Reduce the heat, cover, and simmer for 10 minutes, stirring occasionally to prevent the pasta shapes sticking together.

3 Season with salt and pepper to taste. Transfer the soup to a warm tureen or individual bowls and sprinkle with Parmesan cheese, if using. Serve with fresh crusty bread.

NUTRITION
Calories *295*; Sugars *8 g*; Protein *25 g*;
Carbohydrate *29 g*; Fat *10 g*; Saturates *2 g*

 easy
10 mins
20 mins

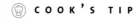 **COOK'S TIP**

Broccoli flowerets can be used to replace the cauliflower flowerets. Substitute 2 tablespoons chopped fresh mixed herbs for the dried mixed herbs.

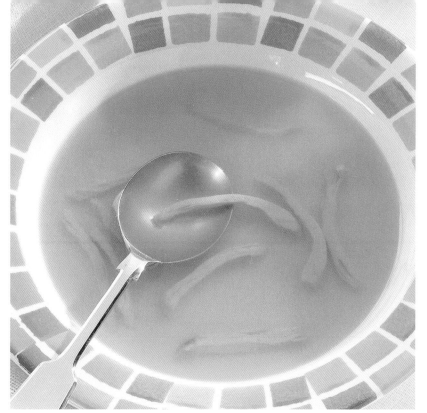

This is a very flavorful soup, especially if you make it from real chicken bouillon. Egg shells and whites are used to give it a crystal-clear appearance.

Chicken Consommé

1 Place the chicken bouillon and sherry in a large pan and heat very gently for 5 minutes.

2 Add the egg whites and the egg shells to the chicken bouillon and whisk until the mixture begins to boil.

3 Remove the pan from the heat and let the mixture stand for 10 minutes. Repeat this process 3 times. This allows the egg white to trap the sediments in the chicken bouillon to clarify the soup. Let the consommé cool for 5 minutes.

4 Carefully place a piece of fine cheesecloth over a pan. Ladle the soup over the cheesecloth and strain into the pan.

5 Repeat this process twice, then gently reheat the consommé. Season with salt and pepper to taste and add the cooked chicken slices. Pour the soup into a warm tureen or individual bowls.

SERVES 8 – 10

8 cups chicken bouillon
²⁄₃ cup medium sherry
4 egg whites, plus egg shells
4 oz/115 g cooked chicken, sliced thinly
salt and pepper

NUTRITION
Calories *96*; Sugars *1 g*; Protein *11 g*;
Carbohydrate *1 g*; Fat *1 g*; Saturates *0.4 g*

✪✪✪✪   challenging

🕐   1 hr 15 mins

🕐   15 mins

 COOK'S TIP

Consommé is usually garnished with freshly cooked pasta shapes, noodles, rice, or lightly cooked vegetables. Alternatively, you could garnish it with omelet strips, drained first on paper towels.

This spicy soup was brought to the West by army and service personnel returning from India. It is perfect for a cold day.

Spicy Mulligatawny Soup

SERVES 4

4 tbsp butter
1 onion, sliced
1 garlic clove, chopped finely
1 lb 2 oz/500 g chicken, diced
⅓ cup diced, smoked, rindless bacon
1 small turnip, diced
2 carrots, diced
1 small tart apple, diced
2 tbsp mild curry powder
1 tbsp curry paste
1 tbsp tomato paste
1 tbsp all-purpose flour
5 cups chicken bouillon
⅔ cup heavy cream
salt and pepper
plain rice, to serve
1 tsp chopped fresh cilantro, to garnish

1 Melt the butter in a large pan and cook the onion, garlic, chicken, and bacon for 5 minutes.

2 Add the turnip, carrots, and apple and cook for a further 2 minutes.

3 Blend in the curry powder, curry paste, and tomato paste and sprinkle over the all-purpose flour.

4 Add the chicken bouillon and bring to a boil. Reduce the heat, cover, and simmer over a gentle heat for about 1 hour.

5 Liquidize the soup. Reheat, season with salt and pepper to taste, and gradually blend in the heavy cream. Garnish the soup with cilantro and serve with small bowls of plain rice.

NUTRITION
Calories 502; Sugars 10 g; Protein 31 g;
Carbohydrate 17 g; Fat 35 g; Saturates 20 g

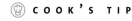

easy

 15 mins

 1 hr 15 mins

(☺) **COOK'S TIP**

This soup may be frozen for up to 1 month; if stored for any longer, the spices may cause it to taste musty.

A hearty soup that is so simple to make, yet packed with flavor. You can use either whole green peas or green or yellow split peas.

Chicken *and* Split Pea Soup

1 Put the bacon, chicken, and onion into a large pan with a little butter and cook over a gentle heat for 8 minutes.

2 Add the peas and the stock to the pan, then bring to a boil. Season with salt and pepper to taste. Reduce the heat, cover and simmer for 2 hours.

3 Stir the heavy cream into the soup. Transfer to a warm tureen or individual soup bowls, sprinkle with parsley and top with cheesy croûtes.

SERVES 6

3 smoked, lean, rindless bacon slices, chopped
2 lb/900 g chicken meat, chopped
1 large onion, chopped
1 tbsp butter
2½ cups ready-soaked split peas
10 cups chicken bouillon
⅔ cup heavy cream
2 tbsp chopped fresh parsley
salt and pepper
cheesy croûtes, to serve

NUTRITION
Calories *443*; Sugars *4* g; Protein *43* g; Carbohydrate *21* g; Fat *21* g; Saturates *11 g*

moderate

10 mins

2 hrs 10 mins

🍳 **COOK'S TIP**

Use 3½ oz/100 g chopped ham instead of the bacon, if preferred.

Tarragon adds a delicate aniseed flavor to this tasty soup. If you can't find tarragon, use parsley for a fresh taste.

Chicken *and* Tarragon Soup

SERVES 4

4 tbsp sweet butter
1 large onion, peeled and chopped
10½ oz/300 g cooked chicken, shredded finely
2½ cups chicken bouillon
1 tbsp chopped fresh tarragon
⅔ cup heavy cream
salt and pepper
sprigs of fresh tarragon, to garnish
deep fried croutons, to serve

1 Melt the butter in a large pan and sauté the onion for 3 minutes.

2 Add the chicken to the pan with 1¼ cups of the chicken bouillon.

3 Bring to the boil, then reduce the heat and simmer for 20 minutes. Allow to cool, then liquidize the soup.

4 Add the remainder of the bouillon and season with salt and pepper to taste.

5 Add the tarragon, pour the soup into a warm tureen or individual serving bowls, and stir in the cream.

6 Garnish the soup with fresh tarragon and serve with deep-fried croutons.

NUTRITION
Calories *434*; Sugars *4 g*; Protein *22 g*; Carbohydrate *6 g*; Fat *36 g*; Saturates *21 g*

easy
10 mins
30 mins

 **COOK'S TIP**

To make garlic croutons, crush 3–4 garlic cloves in a mortar and pestle and add to the oil.

Use the strained vegetables and chicken to make little patties. Simply mash with a little butter, shape them into round cakes, and sauté until golden brown.

Chicken Soup *with* Dumplings

1 Coat the chicken pieces with the flour and season.

2 Melt the butter in a pan and sauté the chicken pieces until lightly browned.

3 Add the oil to the pan and brown the vegetables. Add the sherry and the remaining ingredients, except the bouillon.

4 Cook for 10 minutes, then add the bouillon. Season with salt and pepper to taste and simmer for 3 hours, then strain into a clean pan, and let cool.

5 To make the dumplings, mix together all the dry ingredients in a large, clean bowl. Add the egg, season, and blend in thoroughly, then add enough milk to make a moist dough. Shape into small balls and roll them in a little flour.

6 Cook the dumplings in boiling salted water for 10 minutes.

7 Remove the dumplings carefully with a draining spoon and add them to the soup, then cook for 12 minutes. Transfer the soup to a warm tureen or individual serving bowls, garnished with cilantro, and serve with crusty bread.

SERVES 6

2 lb/900 g chicken meat, sliced
½ cup all-purpose flour
½ cup butter
3 tbsp sunflower oil
1 large carrot, chopped
1 celery stalk, chopped
1 onion, chopped
1 small turnip, chopped
½ cup sherry
1 tsp thyme
1 bay leaf
2 quarts chicken bouillon
salt and pepper
sprigs of fresh cilantro, to garnish
crusty bread, to serve

dumplings
½ cup self-rising flour
1 cup fresh bread crumbs
2 tbsp shredded suet
2 tbsp chopped fresh cilantro
2 tbsp finely grated lemon zest
1 egg

NUTRITION
Calories 578; Sugars 6 g; Protein 39 g;
Carbohydrate 30 g; Fat 32 g; Saturates *16 g*

✪✪✪   moderate

       25 mins

     3 hrs 40 mins

This soup is made with traditional Scottish ingredients. Ideally, it should be left for at least two days before reheating, then served with oatmeal crackers or bread.

Scottish Chicken *and* Barley Broth

SERVES 4

⅓ cup pre-soaked dried split peas
2 lb/900 g skinless chicken, diced
5 cups chicken bouillon
2½ cups water
¼ cup barley, rinsed
1 large carrot, diced
1 small turnip, diced
1 large leek, sliced thinly
1 red onion, chopped finely
salt and white pepper

1 Put the peas and chicken into a pan. Add the bouillon and water and bring slowly to a boil. Skim the bouillon as it boils, using a draining spoon.

2 When all the scum is removed, add the washed barley and simmer for 35 minutes.

3 Add the remaining ingredients and simmer for 2 hours. Season with salt and white pepper to taste.

4 Skim the surface of the soup again and let the broth stand for at least 24 hours. Reheat, adjust the seasoning, and serve.

NUTRITION

Calories 357; Sugars 5 g; Protein 53 g;
Carbohydrate 19 g; Fat 8 g; Saturates 2 g

⭐⭐ easy
🕐 24 hrs 15 mins
🕐 2 hrs 45 mins

 COOK'S TIP

Use either whole-grain barley or pearl barley. Only the outer husk is removed from whole-grain barley and it has a nutty flavor and a chewy texture when cooked.

For a tangy flavor, lemons can be used instead of oranges. This recipe can be adapted to make a duck and orange soup.

Orange, Chicken, *and* Carrot Soup

1 Melt the butter in a large pan. Add the shallots, carrot, celery, and chicken and cook gently for 8 minutes, stirring occasionally.

2 Blanch the orange zest in boiling water for about 3 minutes.

3 Add the orange rind and juice to the pan with the chicken bouillon.

4 Bring slowly to a boil, then reduce the heat and simmer for 50 minutes. Cool the soup, then liquidize in a blender or food processor until smooth.

5 Return the soup to the pan, reheat, season with salt and pepper to taste, and add the cream. Do not boil at this stage or the soup will curdle.

6 Transfer the soup to a warm tureen or individual bowls. Garnish with sprigs of parsley and orange slices and serve with soda bread.

SERVES 4

4 tbsp butter
8 shallots, sliced thinly
2 carrots, sliced thinly
2 stalks celery, thinly sliced
8 oz/250 g skinless chicken breast, chopped finely
finely grated zest and juice of 3 oranges
5 cups chicken bouillon
⅓ cup heavy cream
salt and white pepper
soda bread, to serve

to garnish
sprigs of fresh parsley
orange slices

NUTRITION
Calories *420*; Sugars *16 g*; Protein *18 g*; Carbohydrate *16 g*; Fat *32 g*; Saturates *20 g*

 moderate

15 mins

1 hr 10 mins

🧑‍🍳 **COOK'S TIP**

Use 2 small lemons in place of the oranges. Look for organic or unwaxed oranges or lemons when using zest.

Guinea fowl has a similar texture to chicken, and although it has a milder flavor than other game, it has a slightly stronger taste than chicken.

Chicken *and* Pasta Soup

SERVES 6

1 lb 2 oz/500 g skinless chicken, chopped
1 lb 2 oz/500 g skinless guinea fowl, chopped
2½ cups chicken bouillon
1 small onion
6 peppercorns
1 tsp cloves
pinch of mace
⅔ cup heavy cream
2 tsp butter
2 tsp all-purpose flour
1 cup quick-cook spaghetti, broken into short pieces and cooked
2 tbsp chopped fresh parsley, to garnish

1 Put the chicken and guinea fowl meat into a large pan then add the chicken bouillon.

2 Bring to a boil and add the onion, peppercorns, cloves, and mace. Reduce the heat and simmer gently for about 2 hours, until the bouillon has reduced by one-third.

3 Strain the soup, skim off any fat, and remove any bones from the chicken and guinea fowl.

4 Return the soup and meat to a clean pan. Add the heavy cream and bring to a boil slowly.

5 To make a roux, melt the butter and stir in the flour until it has a pastelike consistency. Add to the soup, stirring until slightly thickened.

6 Just before serving, add the cooked spaghetti.

7 Transfer the soup to a warm tureen or individual serving bowls, garnish with parsley, and serve.

NUTRITION
Calories *418*; Sugars *2 g*; Protein *40 g*;
Carbohydrate *18 g*; Fat *21 g*; Saturates *11 g*

easy

20 mins

2 hrs 15 mins

🎩 **COOK'S TIP**

Instead of spaghetti, use small pasta shapes, such as zite, or macaroni.

This soup is very good made with fresh tomatoes, but you can use canned tomatoes, if preferred.

Fresh Tomato *and* Chicken Soup

1 Melt the butter in a large pan and sauté the onion and chicken for 5 minutes.

2 Add 1¼ cups chicken bouillon to the pan, with the tomatoes and baking soda. Bring the soup to a boil, then reduce the heat and simmer for 20 minutes.

3 Let the soup cool, then blend in a blender or food processor.

4 Transfer the soup to a clean pan and add the remaining chicken bouillon, season with salt and pepper to taste, then add the sugar. Bring to a boil.

5 Transfer the soup to a tureen or individual serving bowls and add a swirl of heavy cream. Garnish with fresh basil leaves and serve.

SERVES 4

4 tbsp sweet butter
1 large onion, chopped
1 lb 2 oz/500 g chicken, shredded very finely
2½ cups chicken bouillon
6 tomatoes, chopped finely
pinch of baking soda
1 tbsp superfine sugar
⅔ cup heavy cream
salt and pepper
sprigs of fresh basil leaves, to garnish

NUTRITION

Calories *481*; Sugars *14 g*; Protein *30 g*; Carbohydrate *15 g*; Fat *34 g*; Saturates *20 g*

 easy

15 mins

 35 mins

 COOK'S TIP

For a healthier version of this soup, use light cream instead of the heavy cream and omit the sugar.

This Chinese-style soup is delicious as an appetizer to an Asian meal or as a light meal in its own right.

Chicken Wonton Soup

SERVES 6

6 cups chicken bouillon
1 tbsp light soy sauce
1 scallion, shredded
1 small carrot, cut into very thin slices

wontons

12 oz/350 g ground chicken
1 tbsp soy sauce
1 tsp grated fresh gingerroot
1 garlic clove, chopped finely
2 tsp sherry
2 scallions, chopped
1 tsp sesame oil
1 egg white
½ tsp cornstarch
½ tsp sugar
about 35 wonton skins

1 Combine all the ingredients for the wonton parcels, except the skins, and mix well.

2 Place a small spoonful of the filling in the center of each wonton skin.

3 Dampen the edges and gather up the wonton skin to form a pouch enclosing the filling.

4 Cook the filled wontons in boiling water for 1 minute, or until they float to the top. Remove with a draining spoon. Bring the chicken bouillon to a boil.

5 Add the soy sauce, scallion, carrot, and wontons to the soup. Reduce the heat and simmer gently for 2 minutes. Transfer the soup to a warm tureen or individual bowls and serve.

NUTRITION

Calories *401*; Sugars *6 g*; Protein *31 g*; Carbohydrate *17 g*; Fat *24 g*; Saturates *13 g*

 easy

20 mins

15 mins

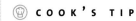 **COOK'S TIP**

Look for wonton skins in Chinese or Asian stores. Fresh skins can be found in the chilled compartment and they can be frozen, if wished. Wrap in plastic wrap before freezing.

A traditional Scottish soup in which a whole chicken is cooked with the vegetables to add a rich flavor to the stock.

Cock-a-leekie Soup

1 Put the chicken, giblets, if using, bouillon, and onion in a large pan. Bring to a boil and skim off any scum that rises to the surface.

2 Add the leeks, allspice, and bouquet garni to the pan, season with salt and pepper to taste. Reduce the heat, cover, and simmer gently for about 1½ hours, until the chicken meat is falling off the bones.

3 Remove the chicken and bouquet garni from the pan and skim any fat from the surface of the soup.

4 Chop the chicken meat and return it to the pan. Add the prunes and bring back to a boil. Reduce the heat and simmer, uncovered, for about 20 minutes. Taste and adjust the seasoning, if necessary, and serve with warm crusty bread.

SERVES 4 – 6

2lb 4 oz–3 lb 5 oz/1–1.5 kg oven-ready
   chicken plus giblets, if available
9 cups chicken bouillon
1 onion, sliced
4 leeks, sliced thinly
pinch of ground allspice or ground coriander
1 bouquet garni, fresh or dried
12 ready-to-eat prunes, halved and pitted
salt and pepper
warm crusty bread, to serve

NUTRITION
Calories *45*; Sugars *4 g*; Protein *5 g*;
Carbohydrate *5 g*; Fat *1 g*; Saturates *0.2 g*

easy

30 mins

2 hrs

COOK'S TIP

You can replace the chicken bouillon with 3 chicken bouillon cubes, dissolved in the same amount of water, if preferred.

Tender cooked chicken strips and baby corn cobs are the main flavors in this delicious clear soup, with just a hint of ginger.

Curried Chicken Soup

SERVES 4

1 cup canned corn, drained
3¾ cups chicken bouillon
12 oz/350 g cooked, skinless chicken, cut into strips
16 baby corn cobs
1 tsp Chinese curry powder
½-inch/1-cm piece of fresh gingerroot, grated
3 tbsp light soy sauce
2 tbsp chopped fresh chives

1 Place the corn in a food processor, with ⅔ cup of the chicken bouillon and process until the mixture forms a smooth purée.

2 Pass the corn purée through a fine strainer, pressing with the back of a spoon to remove any husks.

3 Pour the remaining chicken bouillon into a large pan and add the chicken. Stir in the corn purée to combine well.

4 Add the baby corn cobs and bring the soup to a boil. Boil over medium heat for 10 minutes.

5 Add the Chinese curry powder, ginger, and light soy sauce and stir well to combine. Reduce the heat and simmer for another 10–15 minutes.

6 Stir in the chopped chives. Transfer the soup to a warm tureen or individual soup bowls and serve immediately.

NUTRITION

Calories 206; Sugars 5 g; Protein 29 g; Carbohydrate 13 g; Fat 5 g; Saturates 1 g

easy

10 mins

30 mins

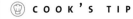 **COOK'S TIP**

Prepare the soup up to 24 hours in advance without adding the chicken. Cool, cover, and store in the refrigerator. Add the chicken and heat the soup through thoroughly before serving.

How delicious a simple, fresh soup can be. Chicken wings are good to use for making the stock, as the meat is very sweet and doesn't dry out.

Chicken Soup *with* Stars

1 Put the chicken in a large, flameproof casserole with the water, celery, carrot, onion, leek, garlic, peppercorns, allspice, herbs, and ½ teaspoon of salt. Bring to a boil and skim off the foam that rises to the surface. Reduce the heat, partially cover, and simmer for 2 hours.

2 Remove the chicken from the bouillon and set aside to cool. Continue to simmer the bouillon, uncovered, for about 30 minutes. When the chicken is cool enough to handle, remove the meat from the bones and, if necessary, cut into bite-size pieces.

3 Strain the stock and remove as much fat as possible. Discard the vegetables and flavorings. (There should be about 7½ cups chicken bouillon.)

4 Bring the bouillon to a boil in a clean pan. Add the pasta and reduce the heat so that the bouillon boils very gently. Cook for about 10 minutes, or until the pasta is tender, but still firm to the bite.

5 Stir in the chicken meat. Adjust the seasoning, if necessary. Transfer the soup to a warm tureen or individual bowls and serve sprinkled with parsley.

SERVES 4

¾ cup small pasta stars, or other very small shapes
chopped fresh parsley, to garnish

chicken bouillon

2 lb 12 oz/1.25 kg chicken pieces, such as wings or legs
11 cups water
1 celery stalk, sliced
1 large carrot, sliced
1 onion, sliced
1 leek, sliced
2 garlic cloves, crushed
8 peppercorns
4 allspice berries
3–4 sprigs of fresh parsley
2–3 sprigs of fresh thyme
1 bay leaf
salt and pepper

NUTRITION

Calories *119*; Sugars *2 g*; Protein *14 g*; Carbohydrate *13 g*; Fat *2 g*; Saturates *0 g*

 moderate

 30 mins

🕐 2 hrs 45 mins

Snacks *and* Appetizers

Since chicken is so versatile and quick to cook, it is perfect for innovative and appetizing snacks. Its unassertive flavor means that it can be enlivened by exotic fruits and spices and Asian ingredients, such as mirin, sesame oil, and fresh ginger. There are fritters, salads, and drumsticks that are stuffed and baked, or served with delicious fruity salsas. As cooked chicken travels well and is easy to eat, many of the following recipes are ideal to take on picnics or to pack into a lunchbox.

Use the breasts from a roasted chicken for this delicious, healthy snack. Served with a mixed salad, it is an ideal light meal for a summer's day.

Jacket Potatoes *with* Chicken

SERVES 4

4 large baking potatoes
9 oz/250 g cooked skinless, boneless chicken breasts, cubed
4 scallions, sliced thickly
1 cup lowfat soft cheese
pepper
mixed salad, coleslaw, or green salad, to serve

1 Scrub the potatoes and prick them all over with a fork. Bake in a preheated oven, 400°F/200°C, for about 60 minutes, until tender, or cook in a microwave on High power for 12–15 minutes.

2 Mix the chicken and scallions with the lowfat soft cheese.

3 Cut a cross into the top of each potato and squeeze slightly apart. Spoon the chicken filling into the potatoes and season with black pepper to taste. Serve immediately with a mixed salad, coleslaw, or green salad.

NUTRITION
Calories *417*; Sugars *4 g*; Protein *28 g*;
Carbohydrate *57 g*; Fat *10 g*; Saturates *5 g*

 very easy
 10 mins
1 hr

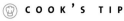 **COOK'S TIP**

Lowfat ricotta cheese, or lowfat fromage blanc can be used as alternatives to soft cheese in this recipe.

These tasty sandwiches are good as a snack on their own or they can be served as part of a picnic.

Open Chicken Sandwiches

1 Reserve the yolk and the white separately from 1 egg.

2 In a large bowl, mix the remaining egg with the butter, English mustard, and anchovy extract, and season with pepper to taste.

3 Mix in the Cheddar and chicken, and spread the mixture on the bread.

4 Make alternate rows of the egg yolk and the egg white on top of the chicken mixture. Arrange the tomato and cucumber slices on top and serve.

SERVES 6

3 hard-cooked eggs, the yolk sieved and the white chopped
2 tbsp butter, softened
2 tbsp English mustard
1 tsp anchovy extract
2 cups grated Cheddar cheese
3 cooked, skinless chicken breasts, chopped finely
6 thick slices of bread or a large French stick cut lengthwise, then cut into 6 pieces and buttered
12 slices each of tomato and cucumber
pepper

NUTRITION
Calories *510*; Sugars *3 g*; Protein *34 g*; Carbohydrate *8 g*; Fat *22 g*; Saturates *18 g*

COOK'S TIP

If you prefer a milder flavor, use a mild mustard. Add mayonnaise, if wished, and garnish with watercress.

 very easy

 15 mins

 0 mins

All the sunshine colors and flavors of the Mediterranean are combined in this easy dish, which would also make a tasty lunch.

Chicken Peperonata

SERVES 4

8 skinless chicken thighs
2 tbsp whole-wheat flour
2 tbsp olive oil
1 small onion, sliced thinly
1 garlic clove, chopped finely
1 each large red, yellow, and green bell
    peppers, seeded and thinly sliced
14 oz/400 g canned chopped tomatoes
salt and pepper
1 tbsp chopped fresh oregano, plus extra
    to garnish
crusty whole-wheat bread, to serve

1 Toss the chicken thighs in the flour.

2 Heat the oil in a wide pan and sauté the chicken quickly until seared and lightly browned, then remove from the pan. Add the onion to the pan and gently sauté until soft. Add the garlic, red, yellow and green bell peppers, tomatoes, and oregano, and bring to a boil, stirring.

3 Arrange the chicken on top of the vegetables, season with salt and pepper to taste. Reduce the heat, cover and simmer for 20–25 minutes, until the chicken is done.

4 Season to taste, garnish with extra oregano, and serve with crusty whole-wheat bread.

NUTRITION
Calories 328; Sugars 7 g; Protein 35 g;
Carbohydrate 13 g; Fat 15 g; Saturates 4 g

easy

15 mins

40 mins

🍴 **COOK'S TIP**

For extra flavor, halve and seed the bell peppers and broil under a preheated broiler until the skins have charred. Let cool and remove the skins. Thinly slice the bell peppers and use in the recipe.

These fritters are delicious served with a mixed salad, a fresh vegetable salsa, or a chili sauce dip.

Chicken *and* Herb Fritters

1 In a large bowl, blend the potatoes, chicken, ham, herbs, and 1 egg, and season with salt and pepper to taste.

2 Shape the mixture into small balls or flat pancakes.

3 Add a little milk to the second egg.

4 Place the bread crumbs on a plate. Dip the balls in the egg and milk mixture and roll in the bread crumbs, to coat them completely.

5 Heat the oil in a large skillet and cook the fritters until golden brown. Garnish with fresh parsley and serve with a mixed salad.

M A K E S 8

1 lb 2 oz/500 g mashed potato, with butter added
1⅓ cups cooked chicken, chopped
⅔ cups cooked ham, chopped finely
1 tbsp fresh mixed herbs
2 eggs, lightly beaten
salt and pepper
milk
2 cups fresh brown bread crumbs
oil, for shallow-frying
sprigs of fresh parsley, to garnish
mixed salad, to serve

N U T R I T I O N
Calories *333*; Sugars *1 g*; Protein *16 g*; Carbohydrate *17 g*; Fat *23 g*; Saturates *5 g*

  easy
  25 mins
  20 mins

🍳 C O O K ' S T I P

To make a tomato sauce to serve with the fritters, heat ¾ cup sieved tomatoes and 4 tablespoons dry white wine. Season, remove from the heat, and add 4 tablespoons plain yogurt. Heat and add chili powder to taste.

A lowfat chicken recipe
with a refreshingly light,
mustard-spiced dip, which
is ideal for a healthy
lunchbox or a light meal
with salad.

Baked Chicken *with* Rosemary

SERVES 4

¹⁄₃ cup rolled oats
1 tbsp chopped fresh rosemary
4 skinless chicken quarters
1 egg white
½ cup natural lowfat fromage blanc
2 tsp whole-grain mustard
salt and pepper
grated carrot salad, to serve

1 Mix together the rolled oats and fresh rosemary, and season with salt and pepper to taste.

2 Brush each piece of chicken with the egg white, then coat in the oat mixture. Place on a cookie sheet and bake in a preheated oven, 400°F/200°C, for 40 minutes, or until the juices run clear, not pink, when the chicken is pierced in the thickest part with a skewer.

3 In a bowl, mix together the fromage blanc and whole-grain mustard, and season again. Serve the chicken, hot or cold, with the carrot salad and mustard dip.

NUTRITION
Calories *120*; Sugars *3 g*; Protein *15 g*;
Carbohydrate *8 g*; Fat *3 g*; Saturates *1 g*

 very easy

10 mins

40 mins

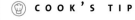 **COOK'S TIP**

Add 1 tablespoon sesame or sunflower seeds to the oat mixture for an even crunchier texture. Experiment with different herbs, instead of the rosemary.

This attractive cold platter makes a delicious addition to a buffet party or a spectacular appetizer for a special meal.

Chicken *and* Herring Platter

1 Spread out the lettuce leaves on a large platter.

2 Arrange the chicken in 3 sections on the platter.

3 Place the rollmops, eggs, and different meats in lines or sections over the remainder of the platter.

4 Use the snow peas, grapes, olives, shallots, almonds, and golden raisins to fill in the spaces between the sections.

5 Grate the zest from the oranges and sprinkle over the whole platter. Peel and slice the oranges and add to the platter with the mint sprig. Season with salt and pepper to taste. Sprinkle with the herring marinade and serve with fresh crusty bread.

SERVES 4

1 large lettuce, leaves separated
4 cooked chicken breasts, sliced thinly
8 rollmop herrings and their marinade
6 hard-cooked eggs, quartered
²/₃ cup cooked ham, sliced
2²/₃ cups cold roast beef, sliced
²/₃ cup cold roast lamb, sliced
1 cup snow peas, cooked
³/₄ cup pitted black grapes,
20 stuffed olives, sliced
12 shallots, boiled
½ cup slivered almonds
⅓ cup golden raisins
2 oranges
sprig of fresh mint, to garnish
salt and pepper
fresh crusty bread, to serve

NUTRITION
Calories *740*; Sugars *62 g*; Protein *88 g*;
Carbohydrate *65 g*; Fat *34 g*; Saturates *9 g*

 moderate

25 mins

 0 mins

(🍳) **COOK'S TIP**

The platter can be served with cold, cooked vegetables, such as green beans, baby corn, and cooked beet, if wished.

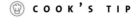

Perfect for a picnic or packed lunch, this Mediterranean-style sandwich can be prepared in advance and wrapped for easy transport.

Mediterranean Pan Bagna

SERVES 6

1 garlic clove, halved
1 large French stick, cut lengthwise
½ cup olive oil
2 oz/55 g cold roast chicken, sliced thinly
2 large tomatoes, sliced
¾ oz/20 g canned anchovy fillets, drained
8 large, pitted black olives, chopped
pepper

1 Rub the garlic over the insides of the bread and sprinkle with the olive oil.

2 Arrange the chicken on top of the bread. Place the tomatoes and anchovies on top of the chicken.

3 Scatter with the black olives, and season with plenty of black pepper. Sandwich the loaf back together and wrap tightly in foil until required. Cut into slices to serve.

NUTRITION
Calories *366*; Sugars *2 g*; Protein *20 g*;
Carbohydrate *20 g*; Fat *23 g*; Saturates *4 g*

⭐ very easy

◐ 10 mins

🕐 0 mins

🍳 **COOK'S TIP**

Arrange a few fresh basil leaves in between the tomato slices to add a warm, aromatic flavor. Use a good-quality olive oil in this recipe for extra flavor.

This classic salad is good as an appetizer or as part of a buffet. Mango chutney makes a tasty addition.

Coronation Chicken

1 Heat the oil in a large skillet and add the chicken, bacon, shallots, garlic, and curry powder. Cook slowly, stirring, for about 15 minutes.

2 Spoon the mixture into a clean mixing bowl. Allow to cool completely, then season with pepper to taste.

3 Blend the mayonnaise with a little honey, then add the fresh parsley. Toss the chicken in the mayonnaise mixture.

4 Place the chicken in a serving dish, garnish with the grapes, and serve with cold saffron rice.

SERVES **6**

4 tbsp olive oil
2 lb/900 g chicken meat, diced
²/₃ cup diced, rindless, smoked bacon,
12 shallots
2 garlic cloves, chopped finely
1 tbsp mild curry powder
1¼ cups mayonnaise
1 tbsp honey
1 tbsp chopped fresh parsley
pepper
½ cup pitted white grapes, quartered,
    to garnish
cold saffron rice, to serve

NUTRITION
Calories *660*; Sugars *5 g*; Protein *40 g*;
Carbohydrate *7 g*; Fat *53 g*; Saturates *9 g*

 COOK'S TIP

You can use this recipe to fill a jacket potato or as a sandwich filling, but cut the chicken into smaller pieces.

very easy

10 mins

15 mins

This recipe can be made a few days ahead and chilled until needed. A food processor makes light work of blending the ingredients.

Chicken Pots *with* Port

SERVES 6

2½ cups cooked smoked chicken, chopped
pinch each of grated nutmeg and mace
½ cup butter, softened
2 tbsp port
2 tbsp heavy cream
butter, for clarifying (see Cook's Tip)
salt and pepper
sprigs of fresh parsley, to garnish
brown bread slices and fresh butter, to serve

1 Place the smoked chicken in a large bowl with the remaining ingredients, and season with salt and pepper to taste.

2 Pound until the mixture is very smooth or blend in a food processor.

3 Transfer the mixture to individual earthenware pots or one large pot.

4 Cover each pot with buttered baking parchment and weigh down with cans or weights. Chill in the refrigerator for 4 hours.

5 Remove the parchment and cover with clarified butter (see Cook's Tip).

6 Garnish each pot with a sprig of parsley and serve with slices of brown bread.

NUTRITION
Calories *345*; Sugars *1 g*; Protein *18 g*;
Carbohydrate *1 g*; Fat *29 g*; Saturates *19 g*

 easy

 4 hrs 20 mins

0 mins

COOK'S TIP

To make clarified butter: melt 1 cup of butter in a saucepan, skimming off the foam as the butter heats. When melted, remove from the heat and let stand for 4 minutes. Strain through cheesecloth and let cool a little.

Ideal for informal parties, these tasty chicken drumsticks can be prepared in advance. Instead of baking the drumsticks, you could cook them on the barbecue.

Cheesy Garlic Drummers

1 Melt the butter in a pan. Add the garlic and sauté gently, stirring, for 1 minute without browning.

2 Remove the pan from the heat and stir in the parsley, the cheeses, and bread crumbs, and season with salt and pepper to taste.

3 Carefully loosen the skin around the drumsticks.

4 Using a teaspoon, push about 1 tablespoon of the stuffing under the skin of each drumstick. Arrange the drumsticks in a large baking pan.

5 Bake in a preheated oven, 375°F/190°C, for about 45 minutes. Serve hot or cold, garnished with lemon slices and with mixed salad greens.

SERVES 6

1 tbsp butter
1 garlic clove, chopped finely
3 tbsp chopped fresh parsley
½ cup ricotta cheese
4 tbsp grated Parmesan cheese
3 tbsp fresh bread crumbs
12 chicken drumsticks
salt and pepper
lemon slices, to garnish
mixed salad greens, to serve

NUTRITION
Calories 241; Sugars 0 g; Protein 28 g;
Carbohydrate 4 g; Fat 13 g; Saturates 05 g

 moderate

25 mins

50 mins

🍴 **COOK'S TIP**

Freshly grated Parmesan has more flavor than ready-packaged grated Parmesan from stores. Grate only as much as you need and wrap the rest up in foil—it will keep for several months in the refrigerator.

A tasty dish that can be served alone as a snack or to accompany a light soup. It is an exciting variation on plain cheese on toast.

Cheese *and* Chicken Toasts

SERVES 4

2 cups grated crumbly cheese
1⅓ cups cooked chicken, shredded
1 tbsp butter
1 tbsp Worcestershire sauce
1 tsp dry English mustard
2 tsp all-purpose flour
4 tbsp mild beer
4 slices of bread
salt and pepper
1 tbsp chopped fresh parsley, to garnish
cherry tomatoes, to serve

1 Place the crumbly cheese, chicken, butter, Worcestershire sauce, mustard, all-purpose flour, and beer in a small pan. Mix all the ingredients together, then season with salt and pepper to taste.

2 Gently bring the mixture to a boil and remove from the heat immediately.

3 Using a wooden spoon, beat until the mixture becomes creamy in texture. Let it cool.

4 Once the chicken mixture has cooled, toast the bread on both sides and spread with the chicken mixture.

5 Place under a hot broiler and broil until bubbling and golden brown.

6 Garnish with a little parsley and serve with cherry tomatoes.

NUTRITION
Calories *495*; Sugars *2 g*; Protein *35 g*;
Carbohydrate *21 g*; Fat *30 g*; Saturates *2 g*

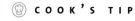

easy

10 mins

10 mins

 COOK'S TIP

This is a variation of Welsh rarebit, which does not traditionally contain chicken. Welsh rarebit topped with a poached egg is called buck rarebit.

This colorful and healthy dish is a variation of a classic salad. Served with crusty brown rolls, it is an ideal light meal for a summer's day.

Waldorf Summer Chicken Salad

1 Place the apples in a bowl with the lemon juice and 1 tablespoon of the mayonnaise. Set aside for 40 minutes.

2 Add the celery, shallots, garlic, and walnuts to the apple and mix together.

3 Stir in the rest of the mayonnaise and blend thoroughly.

4 Add the cooked chicken to the bowl and mix well.

5 Line a glass salad bowl or serving dish with the lettuce leaves. Pile the chicken salad into the center, season with pepper to taste, and garnish with the apple slices.

SERVES 4

1 lb 2 oz/500 g red dessert apples, cored and diced
3 tbsp fresh lemon juice
²/₃ cup light mayonnaise
1 head of celery, sliced thinly
4 shallots, sliced
1 garlic clove, chopped finely
³/₄ cup walnuts, chopped
1 lb 2 oz/500 g cooked chicken, cubed
1 Romaine lettuce, leaves separated
pepper
sliced apple, to garnish

NUTRITION
Calories *471*; Sugars *19 g*; Protein *38 g*;
Carbohydrate *20 g*; Fat *27 g*; Saturates *4 g*

easy

50 mins

0 mins

  COOK'S TIP

Instead of the shallots, use scallions for a milder flavor. Trim the scallions and slice finely.

For this simple, refreshing summer salad you can use leftover roast chicken, or ready-roasted chicken. Add the dressing just before serving, or the spinach will lose its crispness.

Chicken *and* Spinach Salad

SERVES 4

3 celery stalks, sliced thinly
½ cucumber, sliced thinly
2 scallions, sliced thinly
9 oz/250 g young spinach leaves
3 tbsp chopped fresh parsley
12 oz/350 g boneless roast chicken, sliced thinly

dressing

1-inch/2.5-cm piece of fresh gingerroot, grated finely
3 tbsp olive oil
1 tbsp white wine vinegar
1 tbsp honey
½ tsp ground cinnamon
salt and pepper
smoked almonds, to garnish (optional)

1 Toss the celery, cucumber, and scallions in a large bowl with the spinach leaves and parsley.

2 Transfer to serving plates and arrange the chicken on top of the salad.

3 In a screw-topped jar, combine all the dressing ingredients and shake well to mix. Season the dressing with salt and pepper to taste, then pour it over the salad. Sprinkle with a few smoked almonds, if using.

NUTRITION
Calories *225*; Sugars *4 g*; Protein *25 g*;
Carbohydrate *4 g*; Fat *12 g*; Saturates *2 g*

 very easy

10 mins

 0 mins

 **COOK'S TIP**

Fresh young spinach leaves go particularly well with fruit. Try adding a few fresh raspberries or nectarine slices to make a refreshing salad.

The sweetness of the pears complements perfectly the sharp taste of the blue cheese in this delicious warm salad.

Warm Chicken *and* Rice Salad

1 Place the olive oil, shallots, garlic, tarragon, and mustard in a deep bowl. Season with salt and pepper to taste and mix well.

2 Place the chicken in the marinade and turn to coat completely, cover with plastic wrap and chill in the refrigerator for about 4 hours.

3 Drain the chicken, reserving the marinade. Quickly cook the chicken in a large, nonstick skillet for 4 minutes on each side. Transfer the chicken to a warm serving dish.

4 Add the marinade to the pan, bring to a boil, and sprinkle with the flour. Reduce the heat, add the chicken bouillon, apple, and walnuts and gently simmer for 5 minutes. Return the chicken to the sauce, add the heavy cream, and cook for 2 minutes.

5 Mix the salad ingredients together, place on serving plates, and top with a chicken breast and a spoonful of the sauce.

SERVES 6

¼ cup olive oil
6 shallots, sliced
1 garlic clove, chopped finely
2 tbsp chopped fresh tarragon
1 tbsp English mustard
6 skinless, boneless chicken breasts
1 tbsp flour
⅔ cup chicken bouillon
1 dessert apple, cored and diced finely
1 tbsp chopped walnuts
2 tbsp heavy cream
salt and pepper

salad
3½ cups cooked rice
2 large pears, cored and diced
1 cup blue cheese, diced
1 red bell pepper, seeded and diced
1 tbsp chopped fresh cilantro
1 tbsp sesame oil

NUTRITION
Calories *605*; Sugars *13 g*; Protein *41 g*;
Carbohydrate *52 g*; Fat *27 g*; Saturates *10 g*

easy

4 hrs 15 mins

20 mins

CHICKEN

This colorful, simple dish will tempt the appetites of all the family—it is ideal for children, who enjoy the fun shapes of the multi–colored bell peppers.

Harlequin Chicken

SERVES 4

1 tbsp sunflower oil
10 skinless, boneless chicken thighs, cut into bite-size pieces
1 onion, sliced thinly
1 each red, green, and yellow bell peppers, seeded and cut into diamonds
14 oz/400 g canned chopped tomatoes
2 tbsp chopped fresh parsley
pepper

to serve
whole-wheat bread
green salad

1 Heat the oil in a shallow skillet. Add the chicken and onion and sauté quickly until golden.

2 Add the red, green, and yellow bell peppers and cook for 2–3 minutes. Stir in the tomatoes and parsley, and season with pepper to taste.

3 Cover tightly and simmer for about 15 minutes, until the chicken and vegetables are tender. Serve hot with whole-wheat bread and a green salad.

NUTRITION
Calories *183*; Sugars *8 g*; Protein *24 g*; Carbohydrate *8 g*; Fat *6 g*; Saturates *1 g*

 very easy

15 mins

30 mins

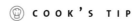 **COOK'S TIP**

If you are making this dish for small children, the chicken can be finely chopped or ground first.

This quick and simple dish is colorful and healthy. It is perfect for an impromptu lunch or supper dish.

Chicken *with* Red *and* Yellow Sauces

1 Heat 1 tablespoon of oil in each of 2 medium-sized pans. Place half the onions, 1 garlic clove, red bell peppers, cayenne pepper, and tomato paste in one pan. Place the remaining onion, garlic, yellow bell peppers, and basil in the other pan.

2 Cover each pan and cook over very low heat for 1 hour, until the bell peppers have softened. If either mixture becomes dry, add a little water. Work each mixture separately in a food processor, then sift separately.

3 Return the separate mixtures to the pans and season with salt and pepper to taste. The 2 sauces can be gently reheated while the chicken is cooking.

4 Put the chicken breasts into a skillet and add the wine and bouillon. Add the bouquet garni and bring the liquid to simmer. Cook the chicken for about 20 minutes, until tender. Remove the bouquet garni.

5 To serve, pour some of each sauce on to individual serving plates. Slice the chicken breasts and arrange on the plates, garnish with fresh herbs.

SERVES 4

2 tbsp olive oil
2 onions, finely chopped
2 garlic cloves, finely chopped
2 red bell peppers, seeded and chopped
good pinch of cayenne pepper
2 tsp tomato paste
2 yellow bell peppers, seeded and chopped
pinch of dried basil
4 skinless, boneless chicken breasts
²/₃ cup dry white wine
²/₃ cup chicken bouillon
bouquet garni, fresh or dried
salt and pepper
fresh herbs, to garnish

COOK'S TIP

If you do not have time to make your own fresh or dried bouquet garni (see page 14), use a bouquet garni herb envelope.

NUTRITION

Calories 257; Sugars 7 g; Protein 29 g; Carbohydrate 8 g; Fat 10 g; Saturates 2 g

moderate

30 mins

1 hr 35 mins

Pâté is easy to make at home, and this combination of lean chicken and ham mixed with herbs is especially straightforward.

Parsley, Chicken, *and* Ham Pâté

SERVES 4

8 oz/225 g cooked skinless, boneless chicken, diced
3½ oz/100 g lean ham, diced
small bunch of fresh parsley
1 tsp grated lime zest, plus extra to garnish
2 tbsp lime juice
1 garlic clove
½ cup lowfat cream cheese
salt and pepper

to serve
lime wedges
crispbread or Melba toast
salad greens

1 Place the chicken and ham in a blender or food processor.

2 Add the parsley, lime zest and juice, and garlic and process until finely ground. (Alternatively, finely chop the chicken, ham, parsley, and garlic and place in a bowl. Gently stir in the lime zest and lime juice.)

3 Transfer the mixture to a bowl and stir in the cream cheese. Season with salt and pepper to taste, cover with plastic wrap, and chill in the refrigerator for about 30 minutes.

4 Spoon the pâté into individual serving dishes and garnish with extra grated lime zest. Serve the pâté with lime wedges, crispbread, and salad greens.

NUTRITION
Calories *119*; Sugars *2 g*; Protein *20 g*;
Carbohydrate *2 g*; Fat *3 g*; Saturates *1 g*

 very easy

45 mins

0 mins

 **COOK'S TIP**

This pâté can be made successfully with other kinds of ground, lean, cooked meat, such as turkey, beef, or pork. Alternatively, replace the meat with peeled shrimp and/or white crabmeat, or with canned tuna in brine, drained.

Cooked potatoes and chicken are combined to make these tasty nutty rissoles, which are served with stir-fried vegetables.

Chicken *and* Almond Rissoles

1 Combine the potatoes, carrot, and chicken with the garlic, herbs, and spices, and season with salt and pepper to taste.

2 Add the egg and bind the ingredients together. Divide the mixture in half and shape into "sausages." Coat each rissole in the nuts. Place the rissoles in a greased ovenproof dish and cook in a preheated oven, 400°F/200°C, for about 20 minutes, until well browned.

3 Heat the peanut oil in a preheated wok or skillet and toss in the vegetables. Cook over high heat for 1–2 minutes, then add the corn cobs and snow peas and cook for another 2–3 minutes. Add the balsamic vinegar.

4 Place the rissoles on serving plates with the stir-fried vegetables. Garnish with lime wedges.

SERVES 4

4 oz/115 g parboiled potatoes, grated
1 carrot, grated
4 oz/115 g cooked chicken, chopped finely or ground
1 garlic clove, crushed
½ tsp dried tarragon or thyme
pinch of ground allspice or ground coriander
1 egg yolk or ½ egg, beaten
¼ cup sliced almonds, finely chopped
salt and pepper
lime wedges, to garnish

stir-fried vegetables
1 tbsp peanut oil
1 celery stalk, sliced thinly diagonally
2 scallions, sliced thinly diagonally
8 baby corn cobs
1½ oz/40 g snow peas or sugar snap peas
2 tsp balsamic vinegar

NUTRITION
Calories *161*; Sugars *3 g*; Protein *12 g*; Carbohydrate *8 g*; Fat *9 g*; Saturates *1 g*

✪✪✪   moderate
     35 mins
    30 mins

Quick Dishes

One of the marvelous qualities of chicken is that when it is cut into small pieces, it can be cooked very quickly, which is welcome for those of us who are too busy to spend a lot of time preparing meals. Pasta makes a perfect partner for chicken as it is also quick to cook—Italian Chicken Spirals look impressive and will fool guests into thinking that you have spent hours slaving away in the kitchen. Chicken breasts are also cooked with a delicious basil, hazelnut, and garlic filling and then served on a bed of pasta, olives, and sun-dried tomatoes. Smaller cuts of chicken are also ideal for stir-fries that can be quickly cooked to produce a tender, moist, and flavorful chicken. Peanut Chicken with Noodles is a crunchy stir-fry that is served with thread egg noodles. Risottos are also an excellent choice for when you are in a hurry—this chapter contains two risotto recipes although the variations for risotto are almost endless!

This famous dish is one of many variations of what is perhaps the best known of all Italian risottos.

Chicken Risotto *à la* Milanese

SERVES 4

¹⁄₂ cup butter
2 lb/900 g chicken meat, sliced thinly
1 large onion, chopped
2¹⁄₂ cups risotto rice
2¹⁄₂ cups chicken bouillon
²⁄₃ cup white wine
1 tsp crumbled saffron strands
salt and pepper
¹⁄₂ cup grated Parmesan cheese, to serve

1 Heat 4 tablespoons of the butter in a pan. Sauté the chicken and onion until golden brown.

2 Add the rice, stir well, and cook for 15 minutes.

3 Heat the bouillon until boiling and gradually add to the rice. Add the white wine, and saffron, and season with salt and pepper to taste, then mix well. Simmer gently for 20 minutes, stirring occasionally, and adding more bouillon if the risotto becomes too dry.

4 Leave to stand for a few minutes and just before serving add a little more bouillon and simmer for a further 10 minutes. Serve the risotto, sprinkled with the Parmesan and stir in the remaining butter.

NUTRITION
Calories *857*; Sugars *1 g*; Protein *57 g*;
Carbohydrate *72 g*; Fat *38 g*; Saturates *21 g*

easy

15 mins

1 hr

🍳 **COOK'S TIP**

A risotto should be moist and creamy but have separate grains. The stock is usually added a little at a time, and only when the last addition has been completely absorbed, but it can be added all at once if you are in a rush.

Chicken is surprisingly delicious when combined with fruits, such as grapes or gooseberries, which make a change to the more usual citrus fruits.

Chicken *and* Cream Sauce

1 Heat the butter and sunflower oil in a wide, flameproof casserole or pan and quickly sauté the chicken breasts until golden brown, turning once. Remove the chicken breasts and keep warm.

2 Add the shallots to the casserole and sauté gently until softened and lightly browned. Return the chicken breasts to the casserole.

3 Add the chicken bouillon and cider vinegar, then bring to a boil. Reduce the heat, cover and simmer gently for 10–12 minutes, stirring occasionally.

4 Transfer the chicken to a serving dish. Add the grapes, cream, and nutmeg to the pan. Heat through and season with salt and pepper to taste. Add a little cornstarch to thicken the sauce, if using. Pour the sauce over the chicken and serve.

SERVES 4

1 tbsp butter
1 tbsp sunflower oil
4 skinless, boneless chicken breasts
4 shallots, chopped finely
²/₃ cup chicken bouillon
1 tbsp cider vinegar
1 cup pitless grapes, halved
¹/₂ cup heavy cream
1 tsp freshly grated nutmeg
salt and pepper
cornstarch, for thickening (optional)

NUTRITION
Calories *351*; Sugars *8 g*; Protein *31 g*; Carbohydrate *5 g*; Fat *22 g*; Saturates *12 g*

 easy

 15 mins

30 mins

🍳 **COOK'S TIP**

If desired, add a little dry white wine or vermouth to the sauce in step 3.

A complete main course, which is cooked within 10 minutes. Thread egg noodles are the ideal accompaniment because they can be cooked quickly while the stir-fry sizzles.

Peanut Chicken *with* Noodles

SERVES 4

3 cups dried thread egg noodles
2 tbsp corn oil
1 tbsp sesame oil
8 boneless chicken thighs or 4 breasts, sliced thinly
2 cups zucchini, sliced thinly
1⅓ cups baby corn, sliced thinly
3¾ cups white mushrooms, sliced thinly
1½ cups bean sprouts
4 tbsp smooth peanut butter
2 tbsp soy sauce
2 tbsp lime or lemon juice
½ cup roasted peanuts
pepper
sprigs of fresh cilantro, to garnish

1 Bring a large pan of lightly salted water to a boil and cook the noodles for 3–4 minutes. Drain the noodles.

2 Meanwhile, heat the corn oil and sesame oil in a preheated wok or large skillet and sauté the chicken over a high heat for 1 minute.

3 Add the zucchini, corn, and white mushrooms and stir-fry for 5 minutes.

4 Add the beansprouts, peanut butter, soy sauce, lime juice, and season with pepper, then cook for another 2 minutes.

5 Transfer the noodles to a serving dish, and scatter with the peanuts. Serve with the stir-fried chicken and vegetables, garnished with sprigs of cilantro.

NUTRITION

Calories *563*; Sugars *7 g*; Protein *45 g*; Carbohydrate *22 g*; Fat *33 g*; Saturates *7 g*

 easy

10 mins

15 mins

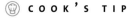 COOK'S TIP

Try serving this stir-fry with rice sticks. These are broad, pale, translucent ribbon noodles made from ground rice.

Chicken breasts are stuffed with creamy ricotta, nutmeg, and spinach, then wrapped in wafer thin slices of prosciutto and gently cooked in wine.

Prosciutto-wrapped Chicken Packets

1 Put the spinach into a strainer and press out any water with a spoon. Mix with the ricotta and nutmeg, and season with salt and pepper to taste.

2 Using a sharp knife, slit each chicken breast through the side and enlarge each cut to form a pocket. Fill with the spinach mixture, reshape the chicken breasts, wrap each breast tightly in a slice of prosciutto, and secure with toothpicks. Cover and chill in the refrigerator.

3 Heat the butter and oil in a skillet and brown the chicken breasts for 2 minutes on each side. Transfer the chicken to a large, shallow ovenproof dish and keep warm until required.

4 Sauté the onions and mushrooms for 2–3 minutes, until lightly browned. Stir in the all–purpose flour, then gradually add the wine and bouillon. Bring to a boil, stirring constantly. Season and spoon the mixture around the chicken.

5 Cook the chicken, uncovered in a preheated oven, 400°F/200°C, for 20 minutes. Turn the breasts over and cook for another 10 minutes. Remove the toothpicks and serve with the sauce, mashed carrots, and green beans.

SERVES 4

½ cup ricotta cheese
pinch of grated nutmeg
4 skinless, boneless chicken breasts, about 6 oz/175 g each
4 prosciutto slices
2 tbsp butter
1 tbsp olive oil
12 small onions or shallots
1½ cups sliced white mushrooms
1 tbsp all-purpose flour
⅔ cup dry white or red wine
1¼ cups chicken bouillon
salt and pepper

to serve
mashed carrots
French beans

NUTRITION
Calories *609*; Sugars *11 g*; Protein *26 g*;
Carbohydrate *45 g*; Fat *38 g*; Saturates *6 g*

  moderate

20 mins

40 mins

These chicken breasts are served with a rich, velvety sauce made from whiskey and plain yogurt.

Chicken Breast *with* Whiskey Sauce

SERVES 6

2 tbsp butter
½ cup shredded leeks
⅓ cup diced carrot
⅓ cup diced celery stalks
4 shallots, sliced
2½ cups chicken bouillon
6 chicken breasts
¼ cup whiskey
scant 1 cup plain yogurt
2 tbsp freshly grated horseradish
1 tsp honey, warmed
1 tsp chopped fresh parsley
salt and pepper
sprigs of fresh parsley, to garnish

to serve
vegetable patties
steamed carrots

1 Melt the butter in a large pan and add the leeks, carrot, celery, and shallots. Cook for 3 minutes, add half of the chicken bouillon, and cook for about 8 minutes.

2 Add the remaining chicken bouillon and bring to a boil. Add the chicken breasts, and cook for 10 minutes.

3 Remove the chicken and slice thinly. Place on a large, hot serving dish and keep warm until required.

4 In another pan, heat the whiskey until reduced by half. Strain the chicken bouillon through a fine strainer, add to the pan, and cook until the liquid has reduced by half.

5 Add the yogurt, horseradish, and honey. Heat gently and add the chopped parsley, and season with salt and pepper to taste. Stir until well blended.

6 Pour a little of the whiskey sauce around the chicken and pour the remaining sauce into a sauceboat to serve.

7 Serve the chicken with vegetable patties made from the leftover vegetables, mashed potato, and fresh vegetables. Garnish with parsley sprigs.

NUTRITION
Calories *337*; Sugars *6 g*; Protein *37 g*;
Carbohydrate *6 g*; Fat *15 g*; Saturates *8 g*

 easy

20 mins

45 mins

Here, chicken is spiked with cayenne pepper and paprika and finished off with a fruity sauce, which is a delicate shade of pink.

Deviled Chicken

1 Mix together the flour, cayenne pepper, and paprika in a bowl and spoon the mixture over the chicken to coat.

2 Shake off any excess flour. Melt the butter in a pan and gently sauté the chicken with the onion for 4 minutes.

3 Stir in the flour and spice mixture. Add the milk slowly, stirring until the sauce has thickened. Simmer until the sauce is smooth.

4 Add the applesauce and grapes and simmer gently for 20 minutes.

5 Transfer the chicken and deviled sauce to a serving dish and top with sour cream and a sprinkling of paprika.

SERVES 2 – 3

¼ cup all–purpose flour
1 tbsp cayenne pepper
1 tsp paprika
12 oz/350 g skinless, boneless chicken, diced
2 tbsp butter
1 onion, chopped finely
1⅞ cups milk, warmed
4 tbsp applesauce
¾ cup white grapes
⅔ cup sour cream
sprinkle of paprika

NUTRITION
Calories 455; Sugars 19 g; Protein 37 g; Carbohydrate 29 g; Fat 23 g; Saturates 14 g

 very easy

10 mins

35 mins

COOK'S TIP

Since paprika is quite a mild spice, you can add more without it becoming too overpowering, if wished.

Steaming allows you to cook these chicken parcels without additional fat, while retaining all the natural juices of the meat.

Italian Chicken Spirals

SERVES 4

4 skinless, boneless chicken breasts
1 cup fresh basil leaves
2 tbsp hazelnuts
1 garlic clove, chopped finely
2 cups dried whole-wheat pasta spirals
2 sun-dried tomatoes or fresh tomatoes, diced
1 tbsp lemon juice
1 tbsp olive oil
1 tbsp capers
½ cup black olives
salt and pepper

1 Beat the chicken breasts with a rolling pin to flatten evenly.

2 Place the basil and hazelnuts in a food processor and process until finely chopped. Mix with the garlic, and season with salt and pepper to taste.

3 Spread the basil mixture over the chicken breasts and roll up from one short end to enclose the filling. Wrap the chicken rolls tightly in foil so that they hold their shape, then seal the ends well.

4 Bring a large pan of lightly salted water to a boil and cook the pasta until tender, but still firm to the bite.

5 Place the chicken packages in a steamer basket or colander set over the pan, cover tightly, and steam for 10 minutes.

6 Drain the pasta and return it to the pan with the lemon juice, olive oil, tomatoes, capers, and olives, then heat through.

7 Pierce the chicken with a skewer to make sure that the juices run clear, not pink, then slice the chicken, arrange over the pasta, and serve.

NUTRITION

Calories 367; Sugars 1 g; Protein 33 g; Carbohydrate 35 g; Fat 12 g; Saturates 2 g

 moderate

 25 mins

 20 mins

🍳 COOK'S TIP

Sun–dried tomatoes have a wonderful, rich flavor, but if you can't find them, use fresh tomatoes instead.

Stuffed with creamy ricotta, spinach, and garlic, the chicken is then gently cooked in a rich tomato sauce. This is a suitable dish to make in advance.

Ricotta-stuffed Chicken *with* Tomato

1 Make a slit between the skin and meat on one side of each chicken breast. Lift the skin to form a pocket, being careful to leave the skin attached to the other side.

2 Put the spinach into a strainer and press out the water with a spoon. Mix with the ricotta, half of the garlic, and season with salt and pepper to taste.

3 Spoon the spinach mixture under the skin of each chicken breast, then secure the edge of the skin with toothpicks.

4 Heat the oil in a skillet, add the onion, and sauté for 1 minute, stirring. Add the remaining garlic and red bell pepper and cook for 2 minutes. Stir in the tomatoes, wine, olives, and seasoning. (Set the sauce aside and chill the chicken if preparing in advance.)

5 Bring the sauce to a boil, pour it into a shallow ovenproof dish and arrange the chicken breasts on top in a single layer.

6 Cook, uncovered, in a preheated oven, 400°F/200°C, for 35 minutes, until the chicken is golden and cooked through. Test by making a slit in one of the chicken breasts with a skewer to make sure the juices run clear, not pink.

7 Spoon a little of the sauce over the chicken breasts, then transfer to serving plates. Serve with pasta.

SERVES 4

4 part-boned chicken breasts
½ cup frozen spinach, defrosted
½ cup ricotta cheese
2 garlic cloves, chopped finely
1 tbsp olive oil
1 onion, chopped
1 red bell pepper, seeded and sliced
14 oz/400 g canned chopped tomatoes
6 tbsp wine or chicken bouillon
10 stuffed olives, sliced
salt and pepper
pasta, to serve

NUTRITION
Calories *316*; Sugars *6 g*; Protein *40 g*;
Carbohydrate *6 g*; Fat *13 g*; Saturates *5 g*

⭐⭐⭐   moderate

🕐   20 mins

🕐   45 mins

Very simple to make and easy to eat with the fingers, this dish can be served warm for a light lunch or cold as part of a buffet.

Chicken Strips *and* Dips

SERVES 2

2 skinless, boneless chicken breasts, cut into thin strips
2 tbsp all–purpose flour
1 tbsp sunflower oil
assorted vegetable sticks, to serve

peanut dip
3 tbsp smooth or crunchy peanut butter
4 tbsp plain yogurt
1 tsp grated orange zest
orange juice (optional)

tomato dip
5 tbsp creamy fromage blanc
1 tomato, chopped
2 tsp tomato paste
1 tsp chopped fresh chives

1 Toss the chicken in the flour to coat.

2 Heat the oil in a nonstick pan and sauté the chicken until golden and thoroughly cooked. Remove the chicken strips from the pan and drain well on paper towels.

3 To make the peanut dip, mix together all the ingredients in a bowl (if liked, add a little orange juice to thin the consistency).

4 To make the tomato dip, mix all the ingredients together in a small bowl.

5 Serve the chicken strips with the dips and a selection of vegetable sticks for dipping.

NUTRITION
Calories 575; Sugars 16 g; Protein 50 g;
Carbohydrate 24 g; Fat 32 g; Saturates 10 g

easy

20 mins

10 mins

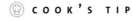 **COOK'S TIP**

For a lowfat alternative, poach the strips of chicken in a small amount of chicken bouillon for 6–8 minutes.

If preferred, use boneless chicken breasts in this recipe. This dish has a surprising combination of coffee and brandy flavors.

Flambéed Chicken

1 Place the chicken breasts or suprêmes on a chopping board, cover with plastic wrap, and pound them until flattened with a meat mallet or rolling pin.

2 Heat the oil in a large skillet and sauté the chicken for 3 minutes on each side. Add the shallots and cook for a further 3 minutes.

3 Sprinkle with the lemon zest and juice and add the Worcestershire sauce and chicken bouillon. Cook for 2 minutes, then sprinkle with the parsley.

4 Add the coffee liqueur and brandy and flame the chicken by lighting the spirit with a taper or long match. Cook until the flame has extinguished and serve.

SERVES 4

4 chicken breasts or suprêmes,
  4½ oz/125 g each
4 tbsp corn oil
8 shallots, sliced
zest and juice of 1 lemon
2 tsp Worcestershire sauce
4 tbsp chicken bouillon
1 tbsp chopped fresh parsley
3 tbsp coffee liqueur
3 tbsp brandy, warmed

NUTRITION
Calories 294; Sugars 5 g; Protein 30 g;
Carbohydrate 6 g; Fat 12 g; Saturates 2 g

 challenging
10 mins
15 mins

COOK'S TIP

A suprême is a chicken fillet that sometimes has part of the wing bone remaining. Chicken breasts can be used instead.

A sweet and fruity glaze coats the chicken breasts in this tasty recipe. The fresh minty rice makes the dish complete.

Golden-glazed Chicken

SERVES 6

6 boneless chicken breasts
1 tsp turmeric
1 tbsp whole-grain mustard
1¼ cups orange juice
2 tbsp honey
2 tbsp sunflower oil
1½ cups long-grain rice
1 orange
3 tbsp chopped fresh mint
salt
sprigs of fresh mint, to garnish

1 With a sharp knife, mark the surface of the chicken breasts in a diamond pattern. Mix together the turmeric, mustard, orange juice, and honey and pour the mixture over the chicken. Chill until required.

2 Remove the chicken from the marinade and pat dry on paper towels.

3 Heat the oil in a wide pan, add the chicken, and sauté until golden, turning once. Drain off any excess oil. Pour the marinade over, cover, and simmer for 10–15 minutes, until the chicken is tender.

4 Boil the rice in lightly salted water until tender and drain well. Finely grate the zest from the orange and stir into the rice with the mint. Adjust the seasoning to taste.

5 Using a sharp knife, remove the peel and white pith from the orange and cut the flesh into segments.

6 Serve the chicken with the orange and mint rice, garnished with orange segments and mint sprigs.

NUTRITION
Calories 427; Sugars 11 g; Protein 39 g;
Carbohydrate 42 g; Fat 12 g; Saturates 3 g

 moderate
 5 mins
 35 mins

🍳 **COOK'S TIP**

To make a slightly sharper flavor, use the grated zest of a small grapefruit instead of the oranges in the rice.

Cooking the chicken in foil parcels makes it aromatic and succulent. It also reduces the amount of oil needed, since the chicken and vegetables cook in their own juices.

Mediterranean Chicken Packages

1 Cut 6 pieces of foil each about 10-inches/25-cm square. Brush the foil squares lightly with oil and set aside until required.

2 With a sharp knife, slash each chicken breast at intervals and place the mozzarella between the cuts in the chicken.

3 Divide the zucchini and tomatoes between the pieces of foil, and season with pepper to taste. Scatter the basil over the vegetables in each package.

4 Place the chicken on top of each pile of vegetables, then wrap in the foil to enclose the chicken and vegetables, tucking in the ends.

5 Place on a cookie sheet and bake in a preheated oven, 400°F/200°C for about 30 minutes.

6 To serve, unwrap each foil package and serve with pasta.

SERVES 6

1 tbsp olive oil
6 skinless chicken breasts
2 cups mozzarella cheese, sliced
3½ cups sliced zucchini
6 large tomatoes, sliced
pepper
1 small bunch of fresh basil or oregano, leaves torn
pasta, to serve

NUTRITION
Calories *234*; Sugars *5 g*; Protein *28 g*;
Carbohydrate *5 g*; Fat *12 g*; Saturates *5 g*

 easy

 25 mins

 30 mins

COOK'S TIP

Place the vegetables and chicken on the shiny side of the foil so the dull surface of the foil is facing outward. This ensures that the heat is absorbed into the package and not reflected away from it.

This quick and healthy stir-fry uses only the minimum of fat. If you don't have a wok, use a wide, heavy-based skillet instead.

Caramelized Chicken Stir-fry

SERVES 4

2 tbsp sunflower oil
4 skinless, boneless chicken breasts, cut into thin strips
1⅓ cups baby corn cobs, halved lengthwise
9 oz/250 g snow peas
1 tbsp sherry vinegar
1 tbsp honey
1 tbsp light soy sauce
1 tbsp sunflower seeds
pepper
egg noodles, to serve

1 Heat the sunflower oil in a preheated wok or large, heavy-based skillet and sauté the chicken over a fairly high heat, stirring constantly, for 1 minute.

2 Add the corn and snow peas and stir-fry over a medium heat for 5–8 minutes, until evenly cooked.

3 Mix together the sherry vinegar, honey, and soy sauce and stir into the pan with the sunflower seeds. Season with pepper to taste. Cook, stirring constantly, for 1 minute. Serve the stir-fry hot with egg noodles.

NUTRITION

Calories *280*; Sugars *7 g*; Protein *31 g*;
Carbohydrate *9 g*; Fat *11 g*; Saturates *2 g*

 very easy

 5 mins

 10 mins

🍳 COOK'S TIP

Rice vinegar or balsamic vinegar make a good substitute for the sherry vinegar.

Served with a creamy tomato sauce, these chicken bites make an excellent light lunch with freshly baked cheesy bread.

Crispy-coated Chicken Morsels

1 In a large, clean bowl, combine the fresh bread crumbs, chicken, leek, mixed herbs, and mustard powder, and season with salt and pepper to taste. Mix together until thoroughly incorporated.

2 Add 1 whole egg and an egg yolk with a little milk to bind the mixture.

3 Divide the mixture into 6 or 8 and shape into thick or thin sausages.

4 Whisk the remaining egg white until frothy. Coat the sausages first in the egg white and then in the crisp bread crumbs.

5 Heat the drippings and sauté the sausages for 6 minutes, until golden brown. Serve with tomatoes and roast potatoes, garnished with parsley.

SERVES **6**

3 cups fresh bread crumbs
9 oz/250 g ground cooked chicken,
1 small leek, chopped finely
pinch each of mixed herbs and mustard powder
2 eggs, separated
4 tbsp milk
crisp bread crumbs, for coating
2 tbsp beef drippings
salt and pepper
sprigs of fresh parsley, to garnish

to serve
tomatoes, halved
roast potatoes

NUTRITION
Calories *268*; Sugars *2 g*; Protein *18 g*;
Carbohydrate *27 g*; Fat *10 g*; Saturates *4 g*

⊛⊛⊛   moderate

   15 mins

   10 mins

🍳 **COOK'S TIP**

If you want to reduce the fat content of this recipe, use a little oil for frying instead of the drippings.

If preferred, long-grain rice can be used instead of risotto rice, but it won't give you the traditional, deliciously creamy texture that is typical of Italian risottos.

Golden Chicken Risotto

SERVES 4

2 tbsp sunflower oil
1 tbsp butter or margarine
1 leek, sliced thinly
1 large yellow bell pepper, seeded and diced
3 skinless, boneless chicken breasts, diced
12 oz/350 g risotto rice
few strands of saffron
6¼ cups chicken bouillon
7 oz/200 g canned corn
½ cup toasted unsalted peanuts
½ cup grated Parmesan cheese
salt and pepper

1 Heat the oil and butter in a large pan. Sauté the leek and yellow bell pepper for 1 minute, then stir in the chicken and cook, stirring, until golden brown.

2 Stir in the rice and cook for 2–3 minutes.

3 Stir in the saffron strands, and season with salt and pepper to taste. Add the bouillon, a little at a time and cook over a low heat, stirring continuously, for about 20 minutes, until the rice is tender and most of the liquid has been absorbed. Do not let the risotto dry out—add more bouillon, if necessary.

4 Stir in the corn, peanuts, and Parmesan cheese, then adjust the seasoning to taste. Serve hot.

NUTRITION

Calories 701; Sugars 7 g; Protein 35 g; Carbohydrate 88 g; Fat 26 g; Saturates 8 g

 easy

10 mins

30 mins

 COOK'S TIP

Risottos can be frozen for up to 1 month, before adding the Parmesan cheese. Remember to reheat the risotto thoroughly as it contains chicken.

This recipe is a chicken version of the classic cottage pie, which is made with ground beef, and is just as delicious. Add the vegetables and herbs of your choice, depending on what you have at hand.

Chicken Cottage Pie

1 Dry-fry the ground chicken, onion, and carrots in a nonstick pan for 5 minutes, stirring frequently.

2 Sprinkle the chicken with the flour and simmer for another 2 minutes.

3 Gradually blend in the tomato paste and bouillon then simmer for 15 minutes. Season with salt and pepper to taste, and add the thyme.

4 Transfer the chicken and vegetable mixture to an ovenproof casserole and let cool.

5 Spoon the mashed potato over the chicken and vegetable mixture and sprinkle with the cheese. Bake in a preheated oven, 400°F/200°C, for 20 minutes, or until the cheese is bubbling and golden, then serve with the peas.

SERVES 4

1 lb 2 oz/500 g ground chicken
1 large onion, chopped finely
2 carrots, diced finely
2 tbsp all-purpose flour
1 tbsp tomato paste
1¼ cups chicken bouillon
pinch of fresh thyme
2 lb/900 g potatoes, mashed with butter and milk and highly seasoned
¾ cup grated crumbly cheese
salt and pepper
peas, to serve

NUTRITION
Calories *496*; Sugars *10 g*; Protein *38 g*; Carbohydrate *52 g*; Fat *17 g*; Saturates *9 g*

 moderate

25 mins

45 mins

 COOK'S TIP

Try using a mixture of cheeses on top of this dish. Choose ones that melt easily to provide a tasty layer of melted cheese on top of the bake.

This unusual recipe uses chicken and Cumberland sausage, cooked in a light batter and served with a rich gravy.

Chicken Toad-in-the-hole Cakes

SERVES 4 – 6

1 cup all-purpose flour
pinch of salt
1 egg, beaten
1 scant cup milk
⅓ cup water
2 tbsp beef drippings
9 oz/250 g chicken breasts, cut into thick chunks
9 oz/250 g pork or beef sausage, cut into chunks

to serve
steamed cabbage
chicken or onion gravy (optional)

1 Mix together the flour and salt in a bowl, make a well in the center, and add the beaten egg.

2 Add half of the milk, and using a wooden spoon, work in the flour slowly. Beat the mixture until smooth, then add the remaining milk and water. Beat again until the mixture is smooth. Let the mixture stand for at least 1 hour.

3 Add the drippings to individual baking pans or to 1 large baking pan. Place a piece of chicken and sausage in each individual pan or arrange several pieces of each in the large pan.

4 Heat in a preheated oven, 425°F/220°C, for 5 minutes, until very hot. Remove the pans from the oven and pour in the batter, leaving space for the mixture to expand as it cooks.

5 Return to the oven and cook for 35 minutes, until risen and golden brown. Do not open the oven door for at least 30 minutes.

6 Serve hot, with cabbage and gravy, if using.

NUTRITION
Calories *470*; Sugars *4 g*; Protein *28 g*;
Carbohydrate *30 g*; Fat *27 g*; Saturates *12 g*

 easy
 1 hr 15 mins
1 hr 15 mins
30 mins

🧑‍🍳 **COOK'S TIP**

Skinless, boneless chicken legs can be used instead of the chicken breast in this recipe. Your favorite variety of flavored sausage can replace the beef or pork sausage, if liked

Low in fat and high in fiber, this colorful casserole makes a healthy and hearty meal. The bread topping soaks up the tasty cooking juices.

Chicken *and* Cannellini Bean Casserole

1 Toss the chicken drumsticks in the flour to coat evenly. Heat the oil in a nonstick pan and sauté the chicken over fairly high heat, turning frequently, until golden brown. Transfer to a large, ovenproof casserole and keep warm until required.

2 Add the onions to the pan and cook for a few minutes until lightly browned. Stir in the garlic.

3 Add the fennel seeds, bay leaf, orange zest and juice, tomatoes, and beans, and season with salt and pepper to taste.

4 Cover tightly and cook in a preheated oven, 375°F/190°C, for 30–35 minutes, until the juices run clear, not pink, when the chicken is pierced through the thickest part with a skewer.

5 For the topping, toss the bread in the oil. Remove the lid from the casserole and top with the bread cubes. Bake for another 15–20 minutes, until the bread is golden and crisp. Serve hot.

SERVES 4

8 skinless chicken drumsticks
1 tbsp whole-wheat flour
1 tbsp olive oil
2 red onions, cut into thin wedges
1 garlic clove, crushed
1 tsp fennel seeds
1 bay leaf
finely grated zest and juice of 1 small orange
14 oz/400 g canned chopped tomatoes
14 oz/400 g canned cannellini or flageolet beans, drained and rinsed
3 thick slices whole-wheat bread, diced
2 tsp olive oil
salt and black pepper

NUTRITION
Calories *345*; Sugars *6 g*; Protein *29 g*; Carbohydrate *39 g*; Fat *10 g*; Saturates *2 g*

 moderate

10 mins

1 hr

COOK'S TIP

Choose beans which are canned in water, with no added sugar or salt. Drain and rinse well before use.

A healthy recipe with a delicate Asian flavor. Use large spinach leaves to wrap around the chicken, but make sure they are young and tender.

Steamed Chicken Parcels

SERVES 4

4 skinless, boneless chicken breasts
1 tsp ground lemongrass
2 scallions, chopped finely
9 oz/250 g young carrots, cut into small batons
9 oz/250 g young zucchini, cut into small batons
2 celery stalks, cut into small batons
1 tsp light soy sauce
9 oz/250 g spinach leaves, rinsed and dried
2 tsp sesame oil
salt and pepper

1 With a sharp knife, make a slit through 1 side of each chicken breast to make a large pocket.

2 Sprinkle the inside of the pocket with lemongrass, and season with salt and pepper to taste. Tuck the scallions into the chicken pockets.

3 Blanch the carrots, zucchini, and celery into a pan of boiling water for 1 minute, drain, and then toss in the soy sauce.

4 Stuff the pockets in each chicken breast with the vegetable mixture, but do not overfill. Fold over firmly to enclose. Reserve the remaining vegetables.

5 Wrap the chicken breasts firmly in the spinach leaves to enclose completely. If the leaves are too firm, steam them gently for a few seconds until they have softened and become flexible.

6 Place the wrapped chicken in a steamer and steam over rapidly boiling water for 20–25 minutes, until tender and done.

7 Stir-fry any leftover vegetable batons and spinach for 1–2 minutes in the sesame oil and serve with the chicken.

NUTRITION
Calories *216*; Sugars *7 g*; Protein *31 g*;
Carbohydrate *7 g*; Fat *7 g*; Saturates *2 g*

✪✪✪✪ challenging

  20 mins

  30 mins

This sweet-sour lemon chicken is delicious hot or cold. Sesame-flavored noodles are the ideal accompaniment for the hot version.

Sweet-sour Chicken

1 Using a sharp knife, score the chicken breast portions with a criss-cross pattern on both sides (making sure that you do not cut all the way through the meat.)

2 Combine the honey, soy sauce, lemon rind and juice in a small bowl, and season with black pepper to taste.

3 Arrange the chicken on the broiler rack and brush with half of the honey mixture. Cook under a preheated broiler for 10 minutes, then turn over and brush with the remaining mixture. Cook for a further 8–10 minutes, until cooked through and tender. The juices should run clear, not pink, when the chicken is pierced in the thickest part with a skewer.

4 Meanwhile, prepare the noodles, according to the instructions on the packet. Drain well and transfer to a warm serving bowl. Add the sesame oil, sesame seeds, and lemon rind and toss well to mix. Season with salt and pepper to taste and keep warm.

5 Serve the chicken with a small mound of noodles, garnished with chopped fresh chives and grated lemon zest.

SERVES 4

4 skinless, boneless chicken breasts, about 4½ oz/125 g each
2 tbsp honey
1 tbsp dark soy sauce
1 tsp finely grated lemon zest
1 tbsp lemon juice
salt and pepper

to garnish
1 tbsp chopped fresh chives
grated lemon zest

to serve
8 oz/225 g rice noodles
2 tsp sesame oil
1 tbsp sesame seeds
1 tsp finely grated lemon zest

NUTRITION
Calories *248*; Sugars *8 g*; Protein *30 g*;
Carbohydrate *16 g*; Fat *8 g*; Saturates *2 g*

easy

5 mins

25 mins

A karahi is an extremely versatile two-handled metal pan, similar to a wok. Food is always cooked over a high heat in a karahi.

Karahi Chicken

SERVES 4

2 tbsp ghee
3 garlic cloves, crushed
1 onion, chopped finely
2 tbsp garam masala
1 tsp ground coriander
½ tsp dried mint
1 bay leaf
1 lb 10 oz/750 g skinless, boneless chicken, diced
scant 1 cup chicken bouillon
1 tbsp chopped fresh cilantro
salt
warm nan bread or chapatis, to serve

1 Heat the ghee in a preheated karahi, wok, or a large, heavy-based skillet. Add the garlic and onion and stir-fry for about 4 minutes, until the onion is golden. Stir in the garam masala, ground coriander, mint, and bay leaf.

2 Add the chicken and cook over high heat, stirring occasionally, for about 5 minutes. Add the bouillon, reduce the heat, and simmer for 10 minutes, until the sauce has thickened and the juices run clear, not pink, when the chicken is pierced with a skewer.

3 Stir in the cilantro and season with salt to taste. Serve immediately with warm nan bread.

NUTRITION
Calories 270; Sugars 1 g; Protein 41 g;
Carbohydrate 1 g; Fat 11 g; Saturates 2 g

 easy

15 mins

20 mins

 COOK'S TIP

Always preheat a karahi or wok before you add the oil to help maintain the high temperature.

This is quite a hot dish, using fresh chiles. If you prefer a milder dish, halve the number of chiles used.

Chile Chicken

1 Place the chicken in a mixing bowl. Add the salt, egg white, cornstarch, and 1 tablespoon of the oil. Turn the chicken in the mixture to coat thoroughly.

2 Heat the remaining oil in a preheated wok or large, heavy-based skillet. Add the garlic and gingerroot and stir-fry for 30 seconds.

3 Add the chicken to the wok and stir-fry for 2–3 minutes, until browned.

4 Stir in the red and green bell peppers, chiles, soy sauce, sherry, and wine vinegar and cook for another 2–3 minutes, until the chicken is done. Transfer to a warm serving dish and serve.

SERVES 4

12 oz skinless, boneless chicken, cut into cubes
½ tsp salt
1 egg white, lightly beaten
2 tbsp cornstarch
4 tbsp vegetable oil
2 garlic cloves, finely chopped
½-inch/1-cm piece of fresh gingerroot, grated
1 red bell pepper, seeded and diced
1 green bell pepper, seeded and diced
2 fresh red chiles, chopped
2 tbsp light soy sauce
1 tbsp dry sherry or Chinese rice wine
1 tbsp wine vinegar

NUTRITION
Calories *265*; Sugars *3 g*; Protein *21 g*;
Carbohydrate *11 g*; Fat *14 g*; Saturates *2 g*

⊗⊗ easy
   10 mins
   10 mins

 COOK'S TIP

When preparing chiles, wear rubber gloves to prevent the seeds from burning and irritating your hands. Be careful not to touch your face, especially your lips or eyes until you have washed your hands.

Casseroles *and* Roasts

Long, slow-cooking means meltingly succulent meat with a good, rich flavor. As chicken does not have a strong flavor, it marries happily with almost any other ingredient, herb, or spice. The recipes in this section are drawn from many cuisines from around the world; there are dishes from Italy, France, Hungary, the Caribbean, and the USA. French classics include Bourguignonne of Chicken and Brittany Chicken Casserole.

The aroma of roasting chicken is always tempting and this section includes the traditional roast, with all the trimmings, as well as many other imaginative cooking ideas. Unusual stuffings to try are zucchini and lime, marmalade, or oat and herb. Many of the recipes in this section exploit the complementary flavors of chicken and fruits, and there are some enticing taste combinations.

Spices, herbs, fruit, nuts, and vegetables are combined to make an appealing casserole with lots of flavor.

Chicken, Almond, *and* Grape Casserole

SERVES 4 – 6

3 tbsp olive oil
2 lb/900 g chicken meat, sliced
10 shallots or baby onions
3 carrots, chopped
½ cup chestnuts, sliced
½ cup slivered almonds, toasted
1 tsp freshly grated nutmeg
3 tsp ground cinnamon
1¼ cups white wine
1¼ cups chicken bouillon
¼ cup white wine vinegar
1 tbsp chopped fresh tarragon
1 tbsp chopped fresh flat-leaf parsley
1 tbsp chopped fresh thyme
grated zest of 1 orange
1 tbsp dark muscovado sugar
¾ cup pitless black grapes, halved
sea salt and pepper
sprigs of fresh herbs, to garnish
wild rice or mashed potato, to serve

NUTRITION

Calories *385*; Sugars *14 g*; Protein *37 g*; Carbohydrate *19 g*; Fat *15 g*; Saturates *2 g*

  easy

 15 mins

2 hrs 15 mins

1 Heat the olive oil in a large pan and sauté the chicken, shallots, and carrots for about 6 minutes, or until browned.

2 Add the remaining ingredients, except the grapes, and simmer over low heat for 2 hours, until the meat is very tender. Stir the casserole occasionally.

3 Add the grapes just before serving. Garnish with herbs and serve with wild rice or mashed potato.

COOK'S TIP

This casserole is delicious served with thick slices of crusty whole-wheat bread to soak up the sauce.

There are many versions of hotchpotch, all using fresh, local, seasonal ingredients. Now, there is an almost endless variety of ingredients available all year, perfect for traditional one-pot cooking.

Chicken *and* Herb Hotchpotch

1 Remove the skin from the chicken quarters, if preferred.

2 Arrange a layer of potato slices in the bottom of a wide casserole. Season with salt and pepper to taste, then add the thyme, rosemary, and bay leaves.

3 Top with the chicken quarters, then sprinkle with the bacon, onion, and carrots. Season well and arrange the remaining potato slices on top, overlapping slightly.

4 Pour the beer over, brush the potatoes with the melted butter, and cover with a lid. Bake in a preheated oven, 300°F/150°C, for about 2 hours, removing the lid for the last 30 minutes to let the potatoes brown. Serve hot.

SERVES 4

4 chicken quarters
6 potatoes, cut into ¼-inch/5-mm thick slices
2 sprigs of fresh thyme
2 sprigs of fresh rosemary
2 bay leaves
1 cup diced, rindless, smoked, lean bacon slices
1 large onion, finely chopped
1 cup carrots, sliced
⅔ cup beer
2 tbsp melted butter
salt and pepper

NUTRITION
Calories *499*; Sugars *6 g*; Protein *43 g*; Carbohydrate *44 g*; Fat *17 g*; Saturates *8 g*

 ✪✪✪   moderate

🕐   15 mins

🕐   2 hrs

🍳 **COOK'S TIP**

This dish is also delicious with stewing lamb, cut into chunks. You can add different vegetables depending on what is in season—try leeks and rutabaga for a slightly sweeter flavor.

The addition of lime juice and zest adds a delicious tangy flavor to this chicken fricassée. The bell peppers add both color and flavor.

Chicken *and* Lime Fricassée

SERVES 4

1 large chicken, cut into small portions
½ cup all-purpose flour, seasoned
2 tbsp oil
1 lb 2 oz/500 g baby onions or shallots, sliced
1 each green and red bell pepper, seeded and sliced thinly
⅔ cup chicken bouillon
juice and zest of 2 limes
2 fresh chiles, chopped
2 tbsp oyster sauce
1 tsp Worcestershire sauce
salt and pepper

1 Coat the chicken pieces in the seasoned flour. Heat the oil in a large skillet and cook the chicken for about 4 minutes, until browned all over.

2 Using a draining spoon, transfer the chicken to a large, deep casserole and sprinkle with the onions. Keep warm until required.

3 Slowly sauté the green and red bell peppers in the juices remaining in the skillet.

4 Add the chicken bouillon, lime zest and juice, and cook for another 5 minutes.

5 Add the chiles, oyster sauce, and Worcestershire sauce. Season with salt and pepper to taste.

6 Pour the bell peppers and juices over the chicken and onions. Cover the casserole with a lid or cooking foil.

7 Cook in the center of a preheated oven, 375°F/190°C, for 1½ hours, until the chicken is very tender, then serve.

NUTRITION
Calories *235*; Sugars *3 g*; Protein *20 g*;
Carbohydrate *26 g*; Fat *6 g*; Saturates *1 g*

moderate

15 mins

1 hr 45 mins

COOK'S TIP

Try this casserole with a cheese biscuit topping. About 30 minutes before the end of cooking time, simply top with rounds cut from cheese biscuit pastry.

A recipe based on a classic French dish. Use a good quality wine when making this casserole and you can serve it to the most discerning diners.

Bourguignonne *of* Chicken

1 Heat the sunflower oil in an ovenproof casserole and brown the chicken all over. Remove from the casserole with a slotted spoon.

2 Add the mushrooms, bacon, shallots, and garlic to the casserole and cook for 4 minutes.

3 Return the chicken to the casserole and sprinkle with flour. Cook for another 2 minutes, stirring.

4 Add the Burgundy wine and chicken bouillon to the casserole and stir until boiling. Add the bouquet garni and season with salt and pepper to taste.

5 Cover the casserole and bake in the center of a preheated oven, 300°F/150°C, for 1½ hours. Remove the bouquet garni.

6 Deep-fry 8 heart-shaped croutons in beef drippings and serve with the bourguignonne and vegetables.

SERVES 4 – 6

4 tbsp sunflower oil
2 lb/900 g chicken meat, diced
3 cups white mushrooms
²⁄₃ cup diced, rindless, smoked bacon slices
16 shallots
2 garlic cloves, crushed
1 tbsp all-purpose flour
²⁄₃ cup white Burgundy wine
²⁄₃ cup chicken bouillon
1 bouquet garni (1 bay leaf, sprigs of fresh thyme, parsley, and sage and 1 celery stalk, tied with string)
salt and pepper

to serve
deep-fried croutons
assorted vegetables

NUTRITION
Calories *476*; Sugars *3 g*; Protein *58 g*; Carbohydrate *8 g*; Fat *21 g*; Saturates *5 g*

 moderate

15 mins

1 hr 30 mins

🍴 COOK'S TIP

A good-quality red wine can be used instead of the white wine, to produce a rich, glossy red sauce.

This economical bake is a complete meal—its crusty, herb-flavored French bread topping mops up the tasty juices, and means there's no need to serve potatoes or rice separately.

Chicken, Bean, *and* Celery Bake

SERVES 4

2 tbsp sunflower oil
4 chicken quarters
16 small whole onions, peeled
3 celery stalks, sliced
14 oz/ 400 g canned red kidney beans, drained and rinsed
4 tomatoes, quartered
scant 1 cup hard cider or chicken bouillon
4 tbsp chopped fresh parsley
1 tsp paprika
4 tbsp butter
12 slices French bread
salt and pepper

1 Heat the oil in a flameproof casserole and sauté the chicken quarters, 2 at a time, until golden. Using a draining spoon, remove the chicken from the pan and set aside until required.

2 Add the onions and sauté, turning occasionally, until golden brown. Add the celery and sauté for 2–3 minutes. Return the chicken to the pan, then stir in the beans, tomatoes, cider or bouillon, and half of the parsley. Season with salt and pepper to taste and sprinkle with the paprika.

3 Cover and cook the chicken in a preheated oven, 400°F/200°C, for 20–25 minutes, until the juices run clear, not pink, when the chicken is pierced in the thickest part with a skewer.

4 Mix the remaining parsley with the butter and spread evenly over the French bread slices.

5 Remove the lid, arrange the bread slices on top so that they are overlapping and bake for another 10–12 minutes, until golden and crisp.

NUTRITION
Calories 736; Sugars 11 g; Protein 50 g; Carbohydrate 55 g; Fat 35 g; Saturates 13 g

easy

15 mins

1 hr

COOK'S TIP

For an Italian-style dish, replace the garlic and parsley bread topping with pesto-covered toasts.

Goulash is traditionally made with beef, but this recipe successfully uses chicken instead. To reduce the fat content, use a lowfat cream in place of the sour cream.

Goulash *with* Claret *and* Cream

1 Toss the chicken in the seasoned flour until it is coated all over.

2 In a flameproof casserole, heat the oil and butter and sauté the onion, shallots, and red and green bell peppers for 3 minutes.

3 Add the chicken and cook for another 4 minutes. Sprinkle with the paprika and rosemary.

4 Add the tomato paste, chicken bouillon, claret, and chopped tomatoes, cover, and cook in the center of a preheated oven, 325°F/160°C, for 1½ hours.

5 Remove the casserole from the oven, let it stand for 4 minutes, add the sour cream, and garnish with parsley.

6 Serve with chunks of bread and salad greens.

 COOK'S TIP

Serve the goulash with buttered ribbon noodles instead of bread. For an authentic touch, try a Hungarian red wine instead of the claret.

SERVES 6

2 lb/900 g chicken meat, diced
½ cup all-purpose flour, seasoned with 1 tsp paprika, salt, and pepper
2 tbsp olive oil
2 tbsp butter
1 onion, sliced
24 shallots, peeled
1 each red and green bell pepper, seeded and chopped
1 tbsp paprika
1 tsp dried rosemary
4 tbsp tomato paste
1¼ cups chicken bouillon
⅔ cup claret
14 oz/400 g canned chopped tomatoes
⅔ cup sour cream
1 tbsp chopped fresh parsley, to garnish

to serve
chunks of bread
salad greens

NUTRITION
Calories 509; Sugars 12 g; Protein 46 g; Carbohydrate 26 g; Fat 32 g; Saturates 10 g

moderate

20 mins

1 hr 45 mins

Root vegetables are always cheap and nutritious, and combined with chicken they make tasty and economical casseroles.

Braised Chicken *with* Dumplings

SERVES 4

4 chicken quarters
2 tbsp sunflower oil
2 leeks, sliced
1 cup carrots, chopped
2 cups parsnips, chopped
2 small turnips, chopped
2½ cups chicken bouillon
3 tbsp Worcestershire sauce
2 sprigs of fresh rosemary
salt and pepper

dumplings
1¾ cups self-rising flour
3½ oz shredded suet
1 tbsp chopped fresh rosemary
cold water, to mix

NUTRITION
Calories *773*; Sugars *14 g*; Protein *46 g*;
Carbohydrate *59 g*; Fat *41 g*; Saturates *15 g*

moderate

25 mins

1 hr 30 mins

1 Remove the skin from the chicken, if preferred. Heat the oil in a large, flameproof casserole or heavy-based pan and sauté the chicken until golden. Using a draining spoon, remove the chicken from the pan. Drain off the excess fat.

2 Add the leeks, carrots, parsnips, and turnips to the casserole and cook for 5 minutes, until lightly colored. Return the chicken to the pan.

3 Add the chicken bouillon, Worcestershire sauce, and rosemary, and season with salt and pepper to taste, then bring to the boil.

4 Reduce the heat, cover and simmer gently for about 50 minutes, or until the juices run clear when the chicken is pierced in the thickest part with a skewer.

5 To make the dumplings, combine the flour, suet, and rosemary leaves with salt and pepper in a bowl. Stir in just enough cold water to bind to a firm dough.

6 Form the dough into 8 small balls and place on top of the chicken and vegetables. Cover and simmer for another 10–12 minutes, until the dumplings are well risen. Serve with the casserole.

This recipe has an Asian
flavor, thanks to the
sesame oil, honey,
and fresh ginger.

Asian Chicken *with* Ginger Sauce

1 Heat the oil in a large skillet. Coat the chicken in the seasoned flour and cook for about 4 minutes, until browned all over. Transfer to a large, deep casserole and keep warm until required.

2 Slowly cook the shallots and mushrooms in the juices.

3 Add the chicken bouillon, Worcestershire sauce, honey, and fresh gingerroot, then season with salt and pepper to taste.

4 Pour the mixture over the chicken, and cover the casserole with a lid or cooking foil.

5 Cook in the center of a preheated oven, 300°F/150°C, for about 1½ hours, until the meat is very tender. Add the yogurt and cook for another 10 minutes. Serve the casserole with a mixture of wild rice and white rice and garnish with fresh parsley.

SERVES 6 – 8

6 tbsp sesame oil
2 lb/900 g chicken meat, cut into bite-size pieces
½ cup all-purpose flour, seasoned
32 shallots, sliced
6 cups wild mushrooms, chopped roughly
1¼ cups chicken bouillon
2 tbsp Worcestershire sauce
1 tbsp honey
2 tbsp grated fresh gingerroot
⅔ cup plain yogurt
salt and pepper
sprigs of fresh flatleaf parsley, to garnish
wild rice and white rice, to serve

NUTRITION
Calories 277; Sugars 6 g; Protein 28 g;
Carbohydrate 17 g; Fat 11 g; Saturates 2 g

 moderate
15 mins
1 hr 50 mins

🍳 **COOK'S TIP**

Mushrooms can be stored in the refrigerator for 24–36 hours. Keep them in paper bags as they "sweat" in plastic. You do not need to peel mushrooms but wild mushrooms must be washed thoroughly.

A tasty way to make chicken joints go a long way, this hearty casserole, spiced with the warm, subtle flavor of ginger, is a good choice for a Halloween party.

Jamaican Hotch–potch

SERVES 4

2 tsp sunflower oil
4 chicken drumsticks
4 chicken thighs
1 onion, thinly sliced
1 lb 10 oz/750 g squash or pumpkin, diced
1 green bell pepper, seeded and sliced
1-inch/2.5-cm piece of fresh gingerroot, finely chopped
14 oz/400 g canned chopped tomatoes
1¼ cups chicken bouillon
¼ cup split lentils
garlic salt and cayenne pepper, to taste
12 oz/350 g canned corn, drained
salt and pepper
crusty bread, to serve

1 Heat the oil in a large, flameproof casserole and sauté the chicken joints until golden, turning frequently.

2 Drain any excess fat from the pan and add the onion, pumpkin, and green bell pepper. Gently sauté for a few minutes until lightly browned. Add the ginger, tomatoes, chicken bouillon, and lentils. Season lightly with garlic salt and cayenne pepper.

3 Cover the casserole and place in a preheated oven, 375°F/190°C, for about 1 hour, until the vegetables are tender and the juices run clear, not pink, if the chicken is pierced in the thickest part with a skewer.

4 Add the corn and cook for a further 5 minutes. Season to taste and serve with crusty bread.

NUTRITION
Calories 277; Sugars 6 g; Protein 33 g;
Carbohydrate 22 g; Fat 7 g; Saturates 1 g

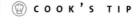

  easy

10 mins

1 hr 15 mins

🍳 COOK'S TIP

If squash or pumpkin is not available, rutabaga makes a good substitute.

Canned borlotti or cannellini beans are both good in this casserole.

Garlic Chicken Casserole

1 Heat the sunflower oil in an ovenproof casserole and sauté the chicken until browned all over. Remove the chicken from the casserole with a draining spoon and set aside until required.

2 Add the mushrooms, shallots, and garlic to the casserole and cook for 4 minutes.

3 Return the chicken to the casserole and sprinkle with the flour, then cook for another 2 minutes.

4 Add the white wine and chicken bouillon, stir until boiling, then add the bouquet garni. Season with salt and pepper to taste.

5 Add the beans to the casserole.

6 Cover and place in the center of a preheated oven, 300°F/150°C, for 2 hours. Remove the bouquet garni and serve the casserole with the squash.

SERVES 4

4 tbsp sunflower oil
2 lb/900 g chicken meat, chopped
3 cups white mushrooms, sliced
16 shallots
6 garlic cloves, chopped finely
1 tbsp all-purpose flour
1 cup white wine
1 cup chicken bouillon
1 fresh bouquet garni, with sage and 1 celery stalk
14 oz/400 g canned borlotti beans, drained and rinsed
salt and pepper
steamed squash, to serve

NUTRITION
Calories 550; Sugars 2 g; Protein 60 g; Carbohydrate 26 g; Fat 19 g; Saturates 4 g

 easy

 10 mins

2 hrs 15 mins

COOK'S TIP

Mushrooms are ideal in a lowfat diet because they are high in flavor and contain no fat. Experiment with the wealth of varieties that are now available from stores.

This is a slow-cooked, old-fashioned stew to warm you up on a cold winter's day. The rarebit toasts are a perfect accompaniment to soak up the rich juices, but if you prefer, serve the stew with jacket potatoes.

Traditional Chicken Stew

SERVES 4 – 6

4 large, skinless chicken thighs
2 tbsp all-purpose flour
2 tbsp English mustard powder
2 tbsp sunflower oil
1 tbsp butter
4 small onions, cut into wedges
2½ cups beer
2 tbsp Worcestershire sauce
salt and pepper
3 tbsp chopped fresh sage leaves

to serve
green vegetables
new potatoes

rarebit toasts
½ cup grated Cheddar cheese,
1 tsp English mustard powder
1 tsp all-purpose flour
1 tsp Worcestershire sauce
1 tbsp beer
2 slices whole-wheat toast

NUTRITION
Calories *476*; Sugars *30 g*; Protein *56 g*;
Carbohydrate *41 g*; Fat *16 g*; Saturates *5 g*

moderate

25 mins

1 hr 45 mins

1 Toss the chicken in the flour and mustard powder to coat evenly. Heat the sunflower oil and butter in a large, flameproof casserole and sauté the chicken over fairly high heat, turning occasionally, until golden. Remove the chicken from the casserole with a draining spoon and keep hot.

2 Sauté the onions until golden. Add the chicken, beer, and Worcestershire sauce, and season with salt and pepper to taste, then bring to a boil. Reduce the heat, cover, and simmer gently for about 1½ hours, until the chicken is very tender.

3 Meanwhile, make the rarebit toasts. Mix the cheese with the mustard powder, flour, Worcestershire sauce, and beer. Spread the mixture over the toasts and cook under a hot broiler for about 1 minute, until melted and golden. Cut the toasts into triangles.

4 Serve the stew with the rarebit toasts, a green vegetable, and new potatoes.

COOK'S TIP

If you do not have fresh sage, use 2 teaspoons of dried sage in step 2.

A hearty, one-dish meal that would make a substantial lunch or supper. As it requires a long cooking time, make double the quantity and freeze half for future use.

Chicken *and* Bean Casserole

1 Cook the chosen beans in salted boiling water for about 25 minutes.

2 Heat the butter and olive oil in a flameproof casserole, add the bacon and chicken, and cook for 5 minutes.

3 Sprinkle with the flour, then add the hard cider and chicken bouillon, stirring constantly to avoid any lumps forming. Season with salt and pepper to taste and bring to a boil.

4 Add the beans, then cover the casserole with a lid or cooking foil and bake in the center of a preheated oven, 325°F/160°C, for 2 hours.

5 About 15 minutes before the end of the cooking time, remove the lid or cooking foil from the casserole.

6 In a skillet, gently cook the shallots and honey together for 5 minutes, turning the shallots frequently.

7 Add the shallots and cooked beet to the casserole and let cook in the oven for the last 15 minutes.

SERVES 6

2½ cups dried beans, such as flageolet, soaked overnight and drained
2 tbsp butter
2 tbsp olive oil
3 rindless bacon slices, chopped
2 lb/900 g chicken pieces
1 tbsp all-purpose flour
1¼ cups hard cider
⅔ cup chicken bouillon
14 shallots
2 tbsp honey, warmed
8 oz/250 g ready-cooked beet
salt and pepper

NUTRITION
Calories 529; Sugars 30 g; Protein 56 g; Carbohydrate 41 g; Fat 16 g; Saturates 5 g

 moderate

24 hrs 15 mins

3 hrs 15 mins

(chef icon) **COOK'S TIP**

To save time, use canned flageolet beans instead of dried. Drain and rinse before adding to the chicken.

A colorful casserole packed with sunshine flavors from the Mediterranean. Sun-dried tomatoes add a wonderful richness and you need very few to make this dish really special.

Rich Chicken Casserole

SERVES 4

8 chicken thighs
2 tbsp olive oil
1 red onion, sliced
2 garlic cloves, crushed
1 large red bell pepper, seeded and
  sliced thickly
thinly pared zest and juice of 1 small
  orange
½ cup chicken bouillon
14 oz/400 g canned chopped tomatoes
½ cup sun-dried tomatoes, sliced thinly
1 tbsp chopped fresh thyme
½ cup pitted black olives
salt and pepper
crusty fresh bread, to serve

to serve
sprigs of fresh thyme
orange zest

1 In a large, heavy-based skillet, sauté the chicken without fat over fairly high heat, turning occasionally until golden brown. Using a draining spoon, drain off any excess fat from the chicken and transfer it to a flameproof casserole.

2 Sauté the onion, garlic, and red bell pepper in the pan over moderate heat for 3–4 minutes. Transfer to the casserole.

3 Add the orange zest and juice, chicken bouillon, canned tomatoes, and sun-dried tomatoes and stir to combine, then bring to a boil.

4 Reduce the heat, cover and simmer gently over low heat for about 1 hour, stirring occasionally. Add the thyme and black olives, then season with salt and pepper to taste.

5 Sprinkle orange zest and thyme over the casserole to garnish, and serve with crusty bread.

NUTRITION
Calories *260*; Sugars *8 g*; Protein *32 g*;
Carbohydrate *8 g*; Fat *11 g*; Saturates *2 g*

moderate
15 mins
1 hr 15 mins

🍲 **COOK'S TIP**

Sun-dried tomatoes have a dense texture and concentrated taste, and add intense flavor to slow-cooked casseroles.

Madeira is a fortified wine, which adds a rich, full flavor to the casserole.

Chicken *and* Madeira Casserole

1 Heat the butter in a large skillet and sauté the onions, carrots, bacon, and mushrooms for 3 minutes, stirring frequently. Transfer to a large casserole dish.

2 Add the chicken to the skillet and cook until browned all over. Transfer to the casserole dish with the vegetables and bacon.

3 Add the white wine and cook until the wine has nearly completely reduced.

4 Sprinkle with the seasoned flour, stirring to prevent any lumps forming.

5 Add the chicken bouillon and bouquet garni, and season with salt and pepper to taste. Cover and cook the casserole for 2 hours. About 30 minutes before the end of the cooking time, add the Madeira wine and continue to cook uncovered. Remove the bouquet garni.

6 Carve the chicken and serve with mashed potato.

SERVES 8

2 tbsp butter
20 baby onions
1½ cups sliced carrots,
1½ cups chopped bacon
3 cups white mushrooms
1 chicken, weighing about 3 lb 5 oz/1.5 kg
1⅞ cups white wine
¼ cup flour, seasoned
1⅞ cups chicken bouillon
bouquet garni, fresh or dried
⅔ cup Madeira
salt and pepper
mashed potato or pasta, to serve

COOK'S TIP

You can add any combination of herbs to this recipe—chervil is a popular herb in French cuisine, but add it at the end of cooking so that its delicate flavor is not lost. Other herbs which work well with chicken are parsley and tarragon.

 moderate

25 mins

2 hrs 40 mins

If you have the time, it is preferable to bone the chicken beforehand or use skinless chicken breasts instead.

Californian Chicken

SERVES 6

6 oz/175 g all-purpose flour
1 tsp paprika
1 tsp freeze-dried Italian seasoning
1 tsp freeze-dried tarragon
1 tsp dried rosemary
2 eggs, beaten
½ cup milk
1 chicken, weighing about 4 lb/1.8 kg, jointed
flour, seasoned
⅔ cup rapeseed oil
2 bananas, quartered
1 apple, cored and cut into rings,
12 oz/350 g canned sweetcorn and bell
    peppers, drained
oil, for frying
mixed salad greens, to serve

1 Mix together the flour, spices, herbs, and a pinch of salt in a large bowl. Make a well in the center and add the eggs.

2 Blend well and slowly add the milk, whisking until very smooth.

3 Toss the chicken pieces in the seasoned flour and dip them into the batter mix.

4 Heat the oil in a large skillet. Add the chicken and fry for about 3 minutes, or until lightly browned all over. Place the chicken on a nonstick cookie tray.

5 Bake the chicken in a preheated oven, 400°F/200°C, for about 25 minutes, until the chicken is tender and golden brown.

6 Meanwhile, batter the bananas and apple rings and fry for 2 minutes, until golden, then remove with a draining spoon.

7 Toss the corn in the leftover batter. Drop spoonfuls of the corn mixture into the oil to make flat patty cakes. Cook for 4 minutes on each side. Keep warm with the apple and banana fritters.

8 Arrange the chicken, corn fritters, and the apple and banana fritters on serving plates. Serve with mixed salad greens.

NUTRITION
Calories *623*; Sugars *13 g*; Protein *45 g*;
Carbohydrate *41 g*; Fat *32 g*; Saturates *4 g*

  moderate

  30 mins

  55 mins

Bacon adds a tasty flavor to this dish. If you can't find fresh garden peas, frozen peas are a very good substitute.

Chicken *and* Green Pea Casserole

1 Melt the butter in a large skillet, add the bacon and onions, and sauté gently for 5 minutes, until lightly browned.

2 Remove the bacon and onions from the pan and set aside until required. Add the chicken pieces to the pan and cook until browned all over. Transfer the chicken to an ovenproof casserole.

3 Add the flour to the pan and cook, stirring until it begins to brown, then slowly blend in the chicken bouillon.

4 Cook the chicken, with the sauce and bouquet garni, in a preheated oven, 400°F/200°C, for 35 minutes.

5 Remove the bouquet garni about 10 minutes before the end of the cooking time and add the peas and the reserved bacon and onions. Stir until combined and season with salt and pepper to taste.

6 When cooked, place the chicken pieces on a large platter, surrounded with the bacon, peas, and onions.

SERVES 4

4 tbsp butter
1 cup diced bacon
16 small onions or shallots
2 lb 4 oz/1 kg skinless, boneless chicken pieces
¼ cup all-purpose flour
2½ cups chicken bouillon
bouquet garni, fresh or dried
4 cups fresh peas
salt and pepper

NUTRITION
Calories *594*; Sugars *6 g*; Protein *77 g*;
Carbohydrate *20 g*; Fat *25 g*; Saturates *9 g*

⭐⭐☆   moderate

     15 mins

1 hr 10 mins

The rich stuffing is cooked under the skin of the chicken, to seal in the flavor and to keep the meat really moist and succulent during cooking.

Festive Apple Chicken

SERVES 6

1 chicken, weighing about 4 lb/1.8 kg
oil, for brushing
2 eating apples, cored and sliced
1 tbsp butter
1 tbsp red currant jelly
salt and pepper
mixed vegetables, to serve

stuffing

1 tbsp butter
1 small onion, chopped finely
¾ cup finely chopped white mushrooms,
½ cup finely chopped smoked ham
½ cup fresh bread crumbs
1 tbsp chopped fresh parsley
1 crisp apple, cored and grated
1 tbsp lemon juice

1 To make the stuffing, melt the butter in a skillet and sauté the onion gently, stirring until softened but not browned. Stir in the mushrooms and cook for 2–3 minutes. Remove from the heat and stir in the ham, bread crumbs, and the parsley.

2 Add the grated apple and lemon juice to the stuffing mixture. Season with salt and pepper to taste.

3 Loosen the breast skin of the chicken and carefully spoon the stuffing mixture under it, smoothing the skin over evenly with your hands.

4 Place the chicken in a roasting pan and brush lightly with oil.

5 Roast the chicken in a preheated oven, 375°F/190°C, for 25 minutes per 1 lb/500 g, plus 25 minutes, or until the juices run clear, not pink, when the chicken is pierced through the thickest part with a skewer. If the breast starts to brown too much, cover the chicken with foil.

6 Sauté the sliced apples in the butter until golden. Stir in the red currant jelly and warm through until melted. Serve the chicken with the apple slices and mixed vegetables.

NUTRITION

Calories *219*; Sugars *7 g*; Protein *29 g*; Carbohydrate *9 g*; Fat *8 g*; Saturates *4 g*

★★★ moderate

🕐 15 mins

🕐 2 hrs 15 mins

The chicken is coated with a fresh-flavored marinade, then roasted. Try serving it with rice, yogurt, and salad.

Cilantro Chicken

1 Place the cilantro, garlic, salt, pepper, lemon juice, and olive oil in a mortar and pestle and pound together or blend in a food processor. Chill the mixture for 4 hours to let the flavors develop.

2 Place the chicken in a roasting pan. Coat generously with the cilantro and garlic mixture.

3 Sprinkle with extra pepper and roast in a preheated oven, 375°F/190°C, on a low shelf for 1½ hours, basting every 20 minutes with the cilantro mixture. If the chicken starts to brown, cover with foil. Carve the chicken, garnish with parsley, and serve with boiled potatoes and carrots.

SERVES 4 – 6

3 sprigs of fresh cilantro, chopped
4 garlic cloves
½ tsp salt
1 tsp pepper
4 tbsp lemon juice
4 tbsp olive oil
1 large chicken
sprigs of of fresh parsley, to garnish

to serve
new potatoes
carrot batons

NUTRITION
Calories *404*; Sugars *0 g*; Protein *47 g*; Carbohydrate *1 g*; Fat *24 g*; Saturates *5 g*

 moderate

4 hrs 10 mins

1 hr 30 mins

 COOK'S TIP

A mortar and pestle is best for pounding small quantities, so as little as possible of the mixture is left in the container.

Chicken goes well with a variety of savory herbs. This combination makes a good partner for tangy feta cheese and rich sun-ripened tomatoes.

Feta Chicken *with* Mountain Herbs

SERVES 4

8 skinless, boneless chicken thighs
2 tbsp each of chopped fresh thyme,
    rosemary, and oregano
1 cup feta cheese, cut into 8 sticks
1 tbsp milk
2 tbsp all-purpose flour
salt and pepper
sugar snap peas, to serve
sprigs of fresh thyme, rosemary,
    and oregano, to garnish

tomato sauce

1 onion, chopped roughly
1 garlic clove, crushed
1 tbsp olive oil
4 plum tomatoes, quartered
sprigs each of fresh thyme, rosemary,
    and oregano

1 Spread out the chicken thighs, smooth side downward.

2 Divide the herbs between the chicken thighs, then place one stick of cheese in the center of each chicken thigh. Season with salt and pepper to taste, then roll up each chicken thigh to enclose the cheese.

3 Place the rolls in an ovenproof dish, brush with milk, and dust with flour to coat evenly.

4 Bake in a preheated oven, 375°F/190°C, for 25–30 minutes, until golden brown and the juices run clear, not pink, when the chicken is pierced in the thickest part with a skewer.

5 To make the sauce, cook the onion and garlic in the olive oil, stirring, until softened and starting to brown.

6 Add the tomatoes, reduce the heat, cover, and simmer for 15–20 minutes, until softened.

7 Add the herbs, then transfer to a food processor and blend to a paste. Press through a strainer to make a smooth, rich sauce. Season and serve the sauce with the chicken and sugar snap peas, garnished with herbs.

NUTRITION

Calories *318*; Sugars *6 g*; Protein *28 g*;
Carbohydrate *15 g*; Fat *17 g*; Saturates *7 g*

 easy

25 mins

 1 hr

Small Squab or Rock Cornish hens are ideal for one or two people, and can be cooked very easily and quickly for a special dinner. If you're preparing this for one, a microwave makes it even quicker and convenient.

Squab *with* Dried Fruits

1 Place the dried fruits in a bowl, cover with the boiling water, and let stand for about 30 minutes.

2 Cut the Squab in half down the breastbone using a sharp knife, or leave them whole, if preferred.

3 Mix the fruit and any juices remaining in the bowl with the walnut halves, honey, and ground allspice and divide the mixture between 2 small roasting bags or squares of foil.

4 Brush the Squab with walnut oil and season with salt and pepper to taste, then place them on top of the fruits.

5 Close the roasting bags or fold the foil over to enclose the Squab and bake on a cookie sheet in a preheated oven, 375°F/190°C, for 25–30 minutes, or until the juices run clear, not pink, when the birds are pierced in the thickest part with a skewer. (To cook in a microwave, use microwave roasting bags and cook on High power for 6–7 minutes each, depending on their size.)

6 Serve with vegetables and new potatoes.

 COOK'S TIP

Alternative dried fruits that can be used in this recipe are cherries, mangoes, or papaya.

SERVES 2

¾ cup ready-to-eat dried apples, peaches, and prunes
½ cup boiling water
2 Squab or Rock Cornish hens
⅓ cup walnut halves
1 tbsp honey
1 tsp ground allspice
1 tbsp walnut oil
salt and pepper

to serve
fresh vegetables
new potatoes

NUTRITION
Calories *316*; Sugars *23 g*; Protein *23 g*; Carbohydrate *23 g*; Fat *15 g*; Saturates *2 g*

easy

40 mins

30 mins

Marmalade lovers will enjoy this festive recipe. You can use any favorite marmalade, such as lemon or grapefruit.

Chicken *with* Marmalade Sauce

SERVES 6

1 chicken, weighing about 5 lb/2.25 kg
sprig of bay leaves
new potatoes, to serve

stuffing
1 celery stalk, chopped finely
1 small onion, chopped finely
1 tbsp sunflower oil, plus extra for brushing
2 cups fresh whole-wheat bread crumbs
4 tbsp marmalade
2 tbsp chopped fresh parsley
1 egg, beaten
salt and pepper

sauce
2 tsp cornstarch
2 tbsp orange juice
3 tbsp marmalade
⅔ cup chicken bouillon
1 orange, segmented
2 tbsp brandy

NUTRITION
Calories *436*; Sugars *20 g*; Protein *45 g*;
Carbohydrate *30 g*; Fat *15 g*; Saturates *4 g*

✪✪✪   moderate

🕐   25 mins

🕐   2 hrs 10 mins

1 Lift the neck flap of the chicken and remove the wishbone using a small, sharp knife. Place a sprig of bay leaves inside the body cavity.

2 For the stuffing, sauté the celery and onion in the oil until softened. Add the bread crumbs, 3 tablespoons of the marmalade, parsley, and egg. Season with salt and pepper to taste and use to stuff the neck cavity of the chicken. Any extra stuffing can be cooked separately.

3 Place the chicken in a roasting pan and brush lightly with oil. Roast in a preheated oven, 375°F/190°C, for 20 minutes per 1 lb 2 oz/500 g, plus 20 minutes or until the juices run clear, not pink, when the chicken is pierced in the thickest part with a skewer. Remove from the oven and glaze with the remaining marmalade.

4 Meanwhile, to make the sauce. Blend the cornstarch in a pan with the orange juice, then add the marmalade and chicken bouillon. Heat gently, stirring, until thickened and smooth. Remove from the heat. Add the orange segments and brandy to the sauce and bring to a boil.

5 Serve the chicken with the orange sauce, any extra stuffing, and new potatoes.

This dish, which uses a partly-boned chicken, is easy to slice and serve. If preferred, stuff in the traditional way and cook any of the remaining stuffing separately.

Glazed Cranberry Chicken

1 To part-bone the chicken, dislocate the legs and place the chicken breast-side downward. Cut a straight line through the skin along the ridge of the back. Scrape the meat down from the bone on both sides.

2 When you reach the point where the legs and wings join the body, cut through the joints. Work around the ribcage until the carcass can be lifted away.

3 For the stuffing, mix the mango with the cranberries, bread crumbs, and mace, then bind with egg. Season with salt and pepper to taste.

4 Place the chicken, skin-side down, and spoon half of the stuffing over. Arrange the bacon rolls down the center, then top with the remaining stuffing. Fold the skin over and tie with string. Turn the chicken over, truss the legs, and tuck the wings underneath. Place in a roasting pan.

5 Mix together the turmeric, honey, and oil, and brush it over the skin.

6 Roast in a preheated oven, 375°F/190°C, for 1½–2 hours, until the juices run clear, not pink, when the chicken is pierced in the thickest part with a skewer. When the chicken starts to brown, cover loosely with foil to prevent overbrowning. Serve the chicken with vegetables.

S E R V E S 4

1 chicken, weighing about 5 lb/2.25 kg
6 slices smoked bacon, each rolled up
½ tsp ground turmeric
2 tsp honey
2 tsp sunflower oil
salt and pepper
seasonal vegetables, to serve

stuffing
1 ripe mango, pitted and diced
¼ cup fresh or frozen cranberries
2 cups bread crumbs
½ tsp ground mace
1 egg, beaten

N U T R I T I O N
Calories *629*; Sugars *10 g*; Protein *61 g*;
Carbohydrate *33 g*; Fat *29 g*; Saturates *8 g*

 challenging

40 mins

1 hr 30 mins

CHICKEN

Chicken suprêmes have a little bit of the wing bone remaining. In this recipe, a tart, fruity sauce perfectly complements the chicken.

Chicken *with* Bacon *and* Red Currants

SERVES 8

4 tbsp butter
juice of 1 lemon
1 cup red currants or cranberries
1–2 tbsp muscovado sugar
8 chicken suprêmes or breasts
16 slices of lean bacon
1 tbsp chopped fresh thyme
4 tbsp beef drippings
4 slices of bread, cut into triangles
salt and pepper
green vegetables, to serve

1 Heat the butter in a pan, add the lemon juice, red currants, and muscovado sugar, and season with salt and pepper to taste. Cook for 1 minute and let cool until required.

2 Meanwhile, season the chicken with salt and pepper. Wrap 2 slices of bacon around each breast and sprinkle with thyme.

3 Wrap each breast in a piece of lightly greased foil and place in a roasting pan. Roast in a preheated oven, 400°F/200°C, for 15 minutes. Remove the foil and roast for another 10 minutes.

4 Heat the drippings in a skillet, add the bread triangles, and sauté on both sides until golden brown.

5 Arrange the chicken with the triangles on large serving plates. Serve with a spoonful of the fruit sauce and a green vegetable.

NUTRITION
Calories *458*; Sugars *7 g*; Protein *42 g*;
Carbohydrate *16 g*; Fat *26 g*; Saturates *12 g*

  moderate

  15 mins

  35 mins

🍴 **COOK'S TIP**

You can use either chopped fresh thyme or dried thyme in this recipe, but remember that dried herbs have a stronger flavor so you only need half the quantity compared to fresh herbs.

The Catalan region of Spain is famous for its wonderful combinations of meat with fruit. Here, peaches lend a touch of sweetness, while the pine nuts, cinnamon, and sherry add an unusual twist.

Spanish Chicken *with* Peaches

1 Combine the bread crumbs with ¼ cup of pine nuts, the egg, and thyme.

2 Remove the skin of the peaches, if necessary. Dice 1 peach into small pieces and stir into the bread crumb mixture. Season with salt and pepper to taste. Spoon the stuffing into the neck cavity of the chicken, securing the skin firmly over it.

3 Place the chicken in a roasting pan. Sprinkle the cinnamon over the skin.

4 Cover loosely with foil and roast in a preheated oven, 375°F/190°C, for 1 hour, basting occasionally.

5 Remove the foil and spoon the sherry over the chicken. Cook for another 30 minutes, basting with the sherry, until the juices run clear when the chicken is pierced in the thickest part with a skewer.

6 Sprinkle the remaining pine nuts over the rest of the peach halves and place in an ovenproof dish. Cook in the oven for the final 10 minutes of the cooking time.

7 Lift the chicken on to a serving plate and arrange the peach halves around it. Skim any fat from the juices, stir in the cream, and heat gently. Serve the sauce with the chicken.

SERVES 6

1 cup fresh brown bread crumbs
½ cup pine nuts
1 small egg, beaten
4 tbsp chopped fresh thyme or 1 tbsp dried thyme
4 fresh peaches, halved or pitted, or 8 canned peach halves
1 chicken, weighing about 5½ lb/2.5 kg
1 tsp ground cinnamon
¾ cup amontillado sherry
4 tbsp heavy cream
salt and pepper

NUTRITION
Calories *586*; Sugars *9 g*; Protein *46 g*; Carbohydrate *14 g*; Fat *36 g*; Saturates *14 g*

  moderate

25 mins

1 hr 30 mins

CHICKEN

This recipe is rather time-consuming but it is well worth the effort. Cherries and chicken make a good flavor combination.

Suprême *of* Chicken *with* Cherries

SERVES **6**

6 large chicken suprêmes
6 black peppercorns, crushed
2 cups pitted black cherries, or canned pitted
    cherries
12 shallots, sliced
4 rindless, lean bacon slices, chopped
8 juniper berries
4 tbsp port
²⁄₃ cup red wine
2 tbsp butter
2 tbsp walnut oil
¼ cup all-purpose flour
salt and pepper

to serve
new potatoes
green beans

1 Place the chicken in an ovenproof dish. Add the peppercorns, cherries, and the shallots.

2 Add the bacon, juniper berries, port, and red wine. Season with salt and pepper to taste.

3 Place the chicken in the refrigerator and leave to marinate for 48 hours.

4 Heat the butter and walnut oil in a large skillet. Remove the chicken from the marinade and sauté quickly in the pan for 4 minutes on each side.

5 Return the chicken to the marinade, reserving the butter, oil, and juices in the pan.

6 Cover the chicken with foil and bake in a preheated oven, 350°F/190°C, for 20 minutes. Transfer the chicken from the baking pan to a warm serving dish. Add the flour to the juices in the skillet and cook for 4 minutes, add the marinade, and bring to a boil. Reduce the heat and simmer for 10 minutes, until the sauce becomes smooth.

7 Pour the cherry sauce over the chicken suprêmes and serve with new potatoes and green beans.

NUTRITION
Calories *363*; Sugars10 *g*; Protein *40 g*;
Carbohydrate *14 g*; Fat *14 g*; Saturates *5 g*

  moderate

  48 hrs 15 mins

1 hr

An unusual change from a plain roast, with a distinctly warming Scottish flavor and a delicious oatmeal stuffing.

Whisky Roast Chicken

1 To make the stuffing, sauté the onion and celery in the butter, stirring over a medium heat until softened.

2 Remove from the heat and stir in the thyme, oatmeal and bouillon, and season with salt and pepper to taste.

3 Stuff the neck end of the chicken with the mixture and tuck the neck flap under. Place in a roasting pan, brush lightly with oil, and roast in a preheated oven, 375°F/190°C, for about 1 hour.

4 Mix the heather honey with 1 tablespoon of the whisky and brush the mixture over the chicken. Return to the oven for a further 20 minutes, or until the chicken is golden brown and the juices run clear, not pink, when the chicken is pierced through the thickest part with a skewer.

5 Lift the chicken on to a serving plate. Skim the fat from the juices, then stir in the flour. Cook over moderate heat, stirring, until the mixture starts to bubble, then gradually add the bouillon and the remaining whisky.

6 Bring to a boil, then reduce the heat and simmer for 1 minute, stirring. Serve the chicken with the sauce, broccoli, and sautéed potatoes.

S E R V E S 6

1 chicken, weighing 4 lb 8 oz/2 kg
oil, for brushing
1 tbsp heather honey
2 tbsp Scotch whisky
2 tbsp all-purpose flour
1¼ cups chicken bouillon
salt and pepper

stuffing

1 onion, finely chopped
1 celery stalk, sliced thinly
1 tbsp butter or sunflower oil
1 tsp dried thyme
4 tbsp oatmeal
4 tbsp chicken bouillon

to serve

broccoli
sautéed potatoes

N U T R I T I O N
Calories *254*; Sugars *6 g*; Protein *27 g*;
Carbohydrate *11 g*; Fat *8 g*; Saturates *2 g*

✪✪✪   moderate

    5 mins

    1 hr 30 mins

This delicious chicken dish has the flavor of roast chicken but unusually it is finished off in a casserole and served with a wild mushroom sauce.

Roast Chicken *with* Wild Mushrooms

SERVES 4

¹⁄₃ cup butter, softened
1 garlic clove, crushed
1 large chicken
2¹⁄₄ cups wild mushrooms
12 shallots
2 tbsp all-purpose flour
²⁄₃ cup brandy, warmed
1¹⁄₄ cups heavy cream
salt and pepper
1 tbsp chopped fresh parsley, to garnish

to serve
roast potatoes
green beans

NUTRITION
Calories *920*; Sugars *4 g*; Protein *50 g*;
Carbohydrate *10 g*; Fat *68 g*; Saturates *38 g*

  moderate

  2 hrs 25 mins

  2 hrs

1 Place the butter and garlic in a bowl. Season with salt and pepper to taste and combine well.

2 Rub the mixture inside the cavity and outside of the chicken and leave for 2 hours.

3 Place the chicken in a large roasting pan and roast in the center of a preheated oven, 450°F/230°C, for 1½ hours, basting with the garlic butter every 10 minutes.

4 Remove the chicken from the roasting pan and set aside to cool slightly.

5 Transfer the chicken juices to a pan and cook the mushrooms and shallots for 5 minutes. Sprinkle with the flour. Add the brandy and ignite using a taper or long match.

6 Add the heavy cream and cook for 3 minutes over a very low heat, stirring all the time.

7 Remove the bones and cut the chicken into small bite-size pieces, then place the meat in a casserole dish. Cover with the mushroom sauce and bake in the oven, with the heat reduced to 325°F/160°C for another 12 minutes. Serve with roast potatoes and French beans, garnished with parsley.

This lowfat recipe is great for summer entertaining, served simply with salad greens and new potatoes. If you spatchcock the chicken (cut it in half and press it flat) you can roast it in under 1 hour.

Honeyed Citrus Chicken

1 Put the chicken on a chopping board with the breast downward. Cut through the bottom part of the carcass using poultry shears or heavy kitchen scissors, making sure not to cut right through to the breast bone.

2 Rinse the chicken with cold water, drain, and place on a board with the skin side uppermost. Press the chicken flat, then cut off the leg ends.

3 Thread 2 long wooden skewers through the bird to keep it flat. Season the skin with salt and pepper to taste.

4 Put all the marinade ingredients in a shallow, nonmetallic dish. Mix well, then add the chicken. Cover and chill for 4 hours, turning the chicken several times.

5 To make the sauce, mix all the ingredients together and season. Spoon into a serving dish, cover, and chill.

6 Transfer the chicken and marinade to a roasting pan, open out the chicken, and place skin-side downward. Tuck the orange wedges around the chicken and roast in a preheated oven, 400°F/200°C, for 25 minutes. Turn the chicken over and roast for another 20–30 minutes. Baste until the chicken is browned and the juices run clear, not pink when it is pierced in the thickest part with a skewer. Garnish with tarragon and serve with the sauce.

SERVES 4

4 lb 8 oz/2 kg chicken
2 oranges, cut into wedges
salt and pepper
sprigs of fresh tarragon, to garnish

marinade
1¼ cups orange juice
3 tbsp cider vinegar
3 tbsp honey
2 tbsp chopped fresh tarragon

sauce
handful of tarragon sprigs, chopped
1 cup fat-free fromage blanc
2 tbsp orange juice
1 tsp honey
½ cup stuffed olives, chopped

NUTRITION
Calories *288*; Sugars *32 g*; Protein *30 g*; Carbohydrate *32 g*; Fat *6 g*; Saturates *1 g*

 challenging

4 hrs 20 mins

55 mins

Beet is one of the most underrated vegetables, adding flavor and color to numerous dishes. Tender young beets are used in this recipe.

Breast *of* Chicken *with* Ham

SERVES 4

4 chicken suprêmes
8 fresh sage leaves
8 thin slices of cooked ham
9oz/250g Stilton or other blue cheese, cut into 8 slices
8 rindless lean bacon slices
²/₃ cup chicken bouillon
2 tbsp port
24 shallots
1 lb 2 oz/500 g baby beets, cooked
1 tbsp cornstarch, blended with a little port
salt and pepper

1 Cut a long slit horizontally along each chicken breast to make a pocket.

2 Insert 2 sage leaves into each pocket and season lightly with salt and pepper.

3 Wrap a slice of ham around each piece of cheese and place 2 into each chicken pocket. Carefully wrap enough bacon around each breast to completely cover the pockets containing the ham and the cheese.

4 Place the breasts in an ovenproof casserole and add the bouillon and port.

5 Add the shallots, cover with a lid or cooking foil and braise in a preheated oven, 375°F/190°C, for about 40 minutes.

6 Carefully place each breast on to a cutting board and slice through them to create a fan effect. Serve them on a warm serving dish with the shallots and beets.

7 Put the juices from the casserole into a pan and bring to a boil, remove from the heat, and add the cornstarch paste. Reduce the heat and simmer the sauce for 2 minutes, then pour it over the shallots and beets.

NUTRITION
Calories 529; Sugars 30 g; Protein 56 g; Carbohydrate 41 g; Fat 16 g; Saturates 5 g

 moderate

25 mins

45 mins

COOK'S TIP

Use any blue cheese, such as Gorgonzola or Roquefort, instead of the Stilton, if preferred.

Squab, or Rock Cornish hens are simple to prepare, and take about 30 minutes to roast. One makes a substantial serving for each person.

Squab *with* Herbs *and* Wine

1 In a bowl, mix together the bread crumbs, one-third of the fromage blanc, and 2 tablespoons each of the parsley and chives. Season with salt and pepper to taste, then spoon the mixture into the neck ends of the birds. Place the birds on a rack in a roasting pan, brush with oil, and season well.

2 Roast in a preheated oven, 425°F/220°C, for 30–35 minutes, until the juices run clear, not pink, when the birds are pierced in the thickest part with a skewer.

3 Place the vegetables in a shallow, ovenproof dish in a single layer and add half of the remaining herbs with the chicken bouillon. Cover and bake for 25–30 minutes, until tender. Strain the vegetables, reserving the cooking juices, and keep warm.

4 Lift the birds on to a serving plate and skim any fat from the juices in the pan. Add the reserved vegetable juices.

5 Blend the cornstarch with the wine and whisk into the sauce with the remaining fromage blanc. Whisk until boiling, then add the remaining herbs. Season to taste. Spoon the sauce over the birds and serve with the vegetables.

SERVES 4

5 tbsp fresh brown bread crumbs
½ cup fromage blanc or plain yogurt
5 tbsp chopped fresh parsley
5 tbsp chopped fresh chives
4 Squab or Rock Cornish hens
1 tbsp sunflower oil
1½ lb/675 g young spring vegetables, such as carrots, zucchini, sugar snap peas, corn, and turnips, cut into small chunks
½ cup boiling chicken bouillon
2 tsp cornstarch
⅔ cup dry white wine
salt and pepper

NUTRITION
Calories *280*; Sugars *7 g*; Protein *32 g*; Carbohydrate *16 g*; Fat *7 g*; Saturates *2 g*

 moderate

20 mins

1 hr 15 mins

It's relatively easy to bone a chicken, but you can ask a friendly butcher to do this for you, if preferred.

Garlic Chicken *with* Mortadella

SERVES 6

1 chicken, weighing about 5 lb/2.25 kg
8 slices mortadella or salami
2 cups fresh white or brown bread crumbs
1 cup grated Parmesan cheese
2 garlic cloves, crushed
6 tbsp chopped fresh basil or parsley
1 egg, beaten
olive oil, for brushing
pepper
spring vegetables, to serve

1 Bone the chicken, keeping the skin intact. Dislocate each leg by breaking it at the thigh joint. Cut down each side of the backbone, taking care not to pierce the breast skin.

2 Pull the backbone clear of the flesh and discard. Remove the ribs, severing any attached flesh with a sharp knife.

3 Scrape the flesh from each leg and cut away the bone at the joint with a knife or shears.

4 Use the bones for a bouillon. Lay out the boned chicken on a board, skin-side down. Arrange the mortadella over the chicken, overlapping slightly.

5 Put the bread crumbs, Parmesan, garlic, and basil in a bowl. Season with pepper to taste and mix well. Stir in the beaten egg to bind the mixture together. Pile the mixture down the middle of the boned chicken, roll the meat around it, and tie securely with fine cotton string.

6 Place in a roasting dish and brush lightly with olive oil. Roast in a preheated oven, 400°F/200°C, for 1½ hours, or until the juices run clear, not pink, when the chicken is pierced in the thickest part with a skewer.

7 Serve hot or cold, in slices, with fresh spring vegetables.

NUTRITION
Calories *578*; Sugars *0.4 g*; Protein *42 g*;
Carbohydrate *9 g*; Fat *42 g*; Saturates *15 g*

 challenging

35 mins

1 hr 30 mins

A cheesy stuffing is tucked under the breast skin of the chicken to give added flavor and moistness to the meat.

Chicken *with* Lime Stuffing

1 To make the stuffing, mix the zucchini with the cheese, lime zest, and bread crumbs, and season with salt and pepper to taste.

2 Carefully ease the skin away from the breast of the chicken.

3 Push the stuffing under the chicken skin with your fingers, to cover the breast evenly.

4 Place the chicken in a baking pan, brush with oil, and roast in a preheated oven, 375°F/190°C, for 20 minutes per 1 lb 2 oz/500 g, plus 20 minutes, or until the juices run clear, not pink, when the chicken is pierced in the thickest part with a skewer.

5 Meanwhile, sauté the zucchini strips in the butter and lime juice until just tender, then serve with the chicken.

SERVES 6

1 chicken, weighing about 5 lb/2.25 kg
oil, for brushing
12oz zucchini, cut into long thin strips
2 tbsp butter
juice of 1 lime
salt and pepper

stuffing
½ cup coarsely grated zucchini
¾ cup medium-fat soft cheese
finely grated zest of 1 lime
2 tbsp fresh bread crumbs

NUTRITION
Calories *236*; Sugars *1 g*; Protein *28 g*;
Carbohydrate *3 g*; Fat *12 g*; Saturates *7 g*

 moderate

15 mins

2 hrs

🍳 **COOK'S TIP**

Finely grate the zucchini, rather than cutting them into strips, to reduce the cooking time.

This colorful, nutritious pot roast makes an ideal family meal or special dinner. Add more vegetables if you're feeding a crowd—if your roasting pot is large enough!

Orange Chicken Pot Roast

SERVES 4

2 tbsp sunflower oil
1 chicken, weighing about 3 lb 2 oz/1.5 kg
2 large oranges
2 small onions, quartered
1lb 2oz/500g small whole carrots or thin carrots, cut into 2-inch/5-cm pieces
⅔ cup orange juice
2 tbsp brandy
2 tbsp sesame seeds
1 tbsp cornstarch
salt and pepper

NUTRITION
Calories 302; Sugars 17 g; Protein 29 g; Carbohydrate 22 g; Fat 11 g; Saturates 2 g

 moderate

 10 mins

2 hrs

1 Heat the oil in a large flameproof casserole and sauté the chicken, turning occasionally, until evenly browned.

2 Cut one orange in half and place half inside the chicken cavity. Place the chicken in a large, deep casserole. Arrange the onions and carrots around the chicken. Season with salt and pepper to taste and add the orange juice.

3 Cut the remaining oranges into thin wedges and tuck them around the chicken among the vegetables.

4 Cover and cook in a preheated oven, 350°F/180°C, for about 1½ hours, or until the juices run clear, not pink, when the chicken is pierced in the thickest part with a skewer, and the vegetables are tender. Remove the lid and sprinkle with the brandy and sesame seeds, then return to the oven for 10 minutes.

5 To serve, lift the chicken on to a large platter. Place the vegetables around the chicken. Skim any excess fat from the juices. Blend the cornstarch with a little cold water, stir it into the juices, and bring to a boil, stirring continuously. Adjust the seasoning, then serve the sauce with the chicken.

🍳 **COOK'S TIP**

Use lemons instead of oranges for a sharper citrus flavor and place a sprig of fresh thyme in the chicken cavity with the lemon half.

Chicken portions are brushed with a classic combination of honey and mustard, then coated in crunchy poppy seeds.

Honey *and* Mustard Baked Chicken

1 Place the chicken pieces, skinless-side down, on a large cookie sheet.

2 Place all the ingredients, except the poppy seeds, in a large bowl and blend together thoroughly. Brush the mixture over the chicken portions.

3 Bake in the center of a preheated oven, 400°F/200°C, for 15 minutes.

4 Carefully turn the chicken pieces over and coat the top side of the chicken with the remaining honey and mustard mixture.

5 Sprinkle the chicken with the poppy seeds and return to the oven for another 15 minutes.

6 Arrange the chicken on a serving dish, pour the cooking juices over, and serve with a tomato and corn salad, if using.

SERVES 4 – 6

8 chicken portions
4 tbsp butter, melted
4 tbsp mild mustard
4 tbsp honey
2 tbsp lemon juice
1 tsp paprika
3 tbsp poppy seeds
salt and pepper
tomato and corn salad, to serve

NUTRITION
Calories *464*; Sugars *17 g*; Protein *64 g*; Carbohydrate *18 g*; Fat *20 g*; Saturates *010 g*

 ⭐⭐ easy

15 mins

30 mins

🍴 **COOK'S TIP**

Mexican rice makes an excellent accompaniment to this dish: boil the rice in vegetable bouillon with fresh chile and vegetables, including onions, tomatoes, garlic, carrots, and peas.

A roast that is full of Mediterranean flavor. A mixture of feta cheese, rosemary, and sun-dried tomatoes is stuffed under the chicken skin.

Mediterranean Roast Chicken

SERVES 6

1 chicken, weighing about 5 lb 8 oz/2.5 kg

sprigs of fresh rosemary, chopped, plus extra for roasting

¾ cup feta cheese, grated coarsely

2 tbsp sun-dried tomato paste

4 tbsp butter, softened

1 bulb garlic, divided into cloves but not peeled

2 lb 4 oz/1 kg new potatoes, halved if large

1 each red, green, and yellow bell pepper, seeded and cut into chunks

3 zucchini, sliced thinly

2 tbsp olive oil

2 tbsp all-purpose flour

2½ cups chicken bouillon

pepper

NUTRITION
Calories *488*; Sugars *6 g*; Protein *37 g*;
Carbohydrate *34 g*; Fat *23 g*; Saturates *11 g*

 moderate

35 mins

2 hrs

1 Carefully cut between the skin and the top of the breast meat using a small pointed knife. Slide a finger into the slit and carefully enlarge it to form a pocket. Continue until the skin is completely lifted away from both breasts and the top of the legs.

2 Mix the rosemary with the feta, sun-dried tomato paste, and butter, and season with pepper to taste, then spoon the mixture under the skin. Put the chicken in a large roasting pan, cover with foil, and cook in a preheated oven, 375°F/190°C, for 20 minutes per 1 lb 2 oz/500 g, plus 20 minutes.

3 Add the vegetables and garlic to the chicken after 40 minutes.

4 Drizzle with oil, tuck in a few stems of rosemary, and season well. Cook for the remaining time, removing the foil for the last 40 minutes of the cooking to brown the chicken.

5 Transfer the chicken to a serving platter. Place some of the vegetables around the chicken and transfer the remainder to a warm serving dish. Remove any fat from the roasting pan and stir the flour into the remaining pan juices. Cook for 2 minutes, then gradually stir in the bouillon. Bring to a boil, stirring until thickened. Strain into a sauce boat and serve with the chicken.

Cheese and mustard make a simple, crispy coating for this quick and healthy dish.

Cheddar-baked Chicken

1 Mix together the milk and mustard in a bowl. In another bowl, combine the cheese, flour, and chives.

2 Dip the chicken into the milk and mustard mixture, brushing to coat evenly.

3 Dip the chicken breasts into the cheese mixture, pressing to coat evenly. Place on a cookie sheet and spoon any spare cheese coating over the top.

4 Bake in a preheated oven, 400°F/200°C, for 30–35 minutes, until golden brown and the juices run clear, not pink, when the chicken is pierced in the thickest part with a skewer. Serve the chicken with jacket potatoes and a mixed salad.

S E R V E S   4

1 tbsp milk
2 tbsp prepared English mustard
1 cup grated sharp hard cheese
3 tbsp all-purpose flour
2 tbsp chopped fresh chives
4 skinless, boneless chicken breasts

to serve
jacket potatoes
mixed salad

N U T R I T I O N
Calories *225*; Sugars *1 g*; Protein *32 g*; Carbohydrate *9 g*; Fat *7 g*; Saturates *3 g*

 COOK'S TIP

There are several varieties of mustard available. For a sharper flavor try French varieties—Meaux mustard has a grainy texture with a warm, spicy flavor, while Dijon mustard is medium-hot and tangy.

very easy

10 mins

35 mins

Any combination of small, young vegetables can be roasted with the chicken, including zucchini, leeks, and onions.

Gardener's Chicken

SERVES 4

1 chicken, weighing about 3 lb 5 oz/1.5 kg
bunch of fresh parsley, plus extra, chopped, to garnish
½ onion
2 tbsp butter, softened
4 tbsp olive oil
1 lb 2 oz/500 g new potatoes
1 lb 2 oz/500 g baby carrots
salt and pepper

stuffing

9oz/250g parsnips, chopped
¾ cup chopped carrots
½ cup fresh bread crumbs
¼ tsp grated nutmeg
1 tbsp chopped fresh parsley

NUTRITION
Calories *674*; Sugars *18 g*; Protein *35 g*;
Carbohydrate *45 g*; Fat *40 g*; Saturates *12 g*

 moderate

15 mins

1 hr 45 mins

1 To make the stuffing, put the parsnips and carrots into a pan, half cover with water, and bring to a boil. Reduce the heat, cover, and simmer until tender. Drain well, then blend in a blender or food processor. Transfer the mixture to a bowl and let cool.

2 Mix in the bread crumbs, nutmeg, and parsley, and season with salt and pepper to taste.

3 Put the stuffing into the neck end of the chicken and push a little under the skin over the breast meat. Secure the flap of skin with a small metal skewer or toothpick.

4 Place the bunch of parsley and onion inside the cavity of the chicken, then place the chicken in a large roasting pan.

5 Spread the butter over the skin and season, cover with foil, and place in a preheated oven, 375°F/190°C, for 30 minutes.

6 Meanwhile, heat the oil in a skillet and lightly brown the potatoes.

7 Transfer the potatoes to the roasting pan and add the baby carrots. Baste the chicken and continue to cook for a further 1 hour, basting the chicken and vegetables after 30 minutes. Remove the foil for the last 20 minutes to allow the skin to crisp. Garnish the vegetables with chopped parsley and serve.

Fresh spring vegetables are the basis of this colorful and filling pot pie, which is topped with hearty whole-wheat dumplings.

Spring-time Chicken Pot Pie

1 Heat the oil in a large, heavy-based pan and fry the chicken, turning occasionally, until golden brown. Drain well and place in a casserole. Add the onion to the pan and cook, stirring occasionally, for 2–3 minutes, until softened.

2 Add the carrots and turnips to the casserole with the onions and beans.

3 Blend the cornstarch with a little of the stock, then stir in the rest, and heat gently, stirring, until boiling. Pour the mixture into the casserole and add the bay leaves. Season with salt and pepper to taste .

4 Cover tightly and bake in a preheated oven, 400°F/200°C, for 50–60 minutes, until the juices run clear, not pink, when the chicken is pierced in the thickest part with a skewer.

5 For the topping, strain the flour and baking powder into a bowl. Mix in the margarine with a fork. Stir in the mustard, cheese, and enough milk to make a fairly soft dough.

6 Roll out and cut 16 rounds with a 1½-inch/4-cm cutter. Uncover the casserole, arrange the dumplings on top of the chicken, then brush with milk, and sprinkle with sesame seeds. Return to the oven and bake for 20 minutes, or until the topping is golden and firm.

SERVES 4

1 tbsp vegetable oil
8 skinless chicken drumsticks
1 small onion, sliced
12 oz/350 g baby carrots, cut into bite-size pieces
2 baby turnips, cut into bite-size pieces
4½ oz/125 g fava beans or peas
1 tsp cornstarch
1¼ cups chicken bouillon
2 bay leaves
salt and pepper

topping
2¼ cups whole-wheat flour
2 tsp baking powder
2 tbsp soft sunflower margarine
2 tsp dry whole-grain mustard
½ cup lowfat sharp Cheddar cheese, grated
skim milk, to mix, plus extra for brushing
sesame seeds, for sprinkling

NUTRITION
Calories *560*; Sugars *10 g*; Protein *389 g*;
Carbohydrate *64 g*; Fat *18 g*; Saturates *4 g*

 moderate

15 mins

1 hr 30 mins

Barbecues *and* Broils

There is nothing more delicious than the juicy flesh and charred skin of chicken that has been grilled over an open fire—after marinating in a flavorsome mixture of oil and herbs, or spices. Try an Asian-style mixture of yogurt and aromatic spices, or soy sauce, sesame oil, and fresh gingerroot. There are some unusual flavors and innovative tastes, including Chicken Kebabs with Blackberry Sauce, and Mediterranean Chicken Kebabs, which are attractive whirls of chicken, bacon, and basil. Squab, or Rock Cornish hens, flavored with lemon and tarragon, are perfect for broiling or barbecue grilling. There is also a recipe for Mint Chicken with Mixed Vegetables, which combines chicken breasts with a selection of broiled vegetables, including zucchini, eggplant, and red bell pepper drizzled with olive oil, and served with crusty bread to soak up the delicious juices.

These spicy chicken wings are good served with a chile salsa and salad. Alternatively, if this is too spicy for your taste, try a sour cream and chive dip.

Chicken Cajun-style

SERVES 4

16 chicken wings
4 tsp paprika
2 tsp ground coriander
1 tsp celery salt
1 tsp ground cumin
½ tsp cayenne pepper
½ tsp salt
1 tbsp oil
2 tbsp red wine vinegar
sprigs of fresh parsley, to garnish

to serve
cherry tomatoes
mixed salad greens
sauce of your choice

1 Remove the wing tips with kitchen scissors.

2 Mix together the paprika, ground coriander, celery salt, ground cumin, cayenne pepper, salt, oil, and red wine vinegar.

3 Rub this mixture over the wings to coat evenly and set aside in the refrigerator for at least 1 hour to allow the flavors to permeate the chicken.

4 Cook the chicken wings under a preheated broiler, occasionally brushing with oil, for about 15 minutes, turning often until done.

5 Garnish the chicken with fresh parsley and serve with cherry tomatoes, mixed salad greens, and the sauce of your choice.

NUTRITION
Calories *430*; Sugars *13 g*; Protein *40 g*;
Carbohydrate *7 g*; Fat *6 g*; Saturates *2 g*

very easy

1 hr 10 mins

15 mins

 **COOK'S TIP**

To save time, you can buy ready-made Cajun spice seasoning to rub over the chicken wings.

This is a quick and easy recipe for the broiler, perfect for lunch or to eat as part of a picnic, because it travels well.

Spicy Sesame Chicken

1 Make cuts in the chicken flesh at intervals with a sharp knife.

2 Combine the plain yogurt, lemon zest and juice, and curry paste in a bowl to make a smooth mixture.

3 Spoon the mixture over the chicken and arrange on a foil-lined broiler pan or cookie sheet.

4 Place the chicken quarters under a preheated medium-hot broiler and broil for 12–15 minutes, turning once, until golden brown and done. Just before the end of the cooking time, sprinkle the chicken with the sesame seeds.

5 Serve with salad greens, nan bread, and lemon wedges.

SERVES 4

4 skinless chicken quarters
½ cup plain yogurt
finely grated zest and juice of 1 small lemon
2 tsp medium-hot curry paste
1 tbsp sesame seeds

to serve
salad greens
nan bread
lemon wedges

NUTRITION
Calories *110*; Sugars *3 g*; Protein *15 g*;
Carbohydrate *3 g*; Fat *4 g*; Saturates *1 g*

 very easy

5 mins

15 mins

🍳 **COOK'S TIP**

Poppy seeds, fennel seeds, or cumin seeds, or a mixture of all these, can also be used to sprinkle over the chicken.

Chicken wings and corn in a sticky ginger marinade are best eaten with the fingers—there's no other way!

Ginger Chicken *and* Corn

SERVES 6

3 fresh corn ears, each cut into 6 slices
12 chicken wings
1-inch/2.5-cm piece of fresh gingerroot, grated or finely chopped
6 tbsp lemon juice
4 tsp sunflower oil
1 tbsp superfine sugar

to serve
jacket potatoes
mixed salad greens

1 Place the corn ear slices in a large bowl with the chicken wings.

2 Mix the gingerroot with the lemon juice, sunflower oil, and sugar, then toss with the corn and chicken to coat.

3 Thread the corn and chicken wings on to metal or presoaked wooden skewers, to make turning easier.

4 Cook the corn and chicken under a preheated medium-hot broiler or grill on the barbecue for 15–20 minutes, basting with the ginger glaze. Turn frequently until the corn is golden brown and tender, and the chicken is done. Serve with jacket potatoes and salad.

NUTRITION
Calories *123*; Sugars *3 g*; Protein *14 g*; Carbohydrate *3 g*; Fat *6 g*; Saturates *1 g*

 very easy

10 mins

20 mins

 **COOK'S TIP**

When you are buying fresh corn, look for plump, tightly packed kernels. If fresh corn is unavailable, you can use thawed frozen corn instead.

Broiling and grilling are quick and healthy cooking methods, ideal for sealing in the juices and flavor of chicken breasts, and a wonderful way to cook vegetables.

Mint Chicken *with* Mixed Vegetables

1 Place the eggplant in a colander and sprinkle with salt. Leave over a bowl to drain for 30 minutes, rinse, and dry. (This will get rid of any bitter juices.)

2 Mix together the garlic, lemon zest, mint, and olive oil, and season with salt and pepper to taste.

3 Slash the chicken breasts at intervals with a sharp knife. Spoon about half of the oil mixture over the chicken and stir to combine.

4 Combine the eggplant and the remaining vegetables, then toss in the remaining oil mixture. Marinate the chicken and vegetables for about 30 minutes.

5 Cook the chicken breasts and vegetables under a preheated hot broiler or barbecue grill, turning occasionally, until golden brown and tender, or cook on a ridged griddle pan on the stove.

6 Brush the bread slices with olive oil and broil until golden.

7 Drizzle a little olive oil over the chicken and grilled vegetables and serve hot or cold with the toasted bread slices.

SERVES **4**

1 small eggplant, sliced
2 garlic cloves, crushed
finely grated zest of ½ lemon
1 tbsp chopped fresh mint
6 tbsp olive oil, plus extra for brushing
4 boneless chicken breasts
2 zucchini, sliced
1 red bell pepper, seeded and quartered
1 small bulb fennel, sliced thickly
1 large red onion, sliced thickly
1 small ciabatta loaf or 1 French baguette, sliced
salt and pepper

NUTRITION
Calories *611*; Sugars *11 g*; Protein *43 g*;
Carbohydrate *66 g*; Fat *21 g*; Saturates *3 g*

✪✪✪ moderate
  1 hr 5 mins
  25 mins

In this recipe, chicken is given a Caribbean flavor. The marinade keeps it moist and succulent during cooking.

Tropical Chicken Skewers

SERVES 6

1 lb 10 oz/750 g skinless, boneless chicken breasts, cut into 1-inch/2.5-cm cubes

2 tbsp medium sherry

3 mangoes, pitted and cut into 1-inch/2.5-cm cubes

bay leaves

2 tbsp oil

2 tbsp coarsely shredded coconut

pepper

salad greens, to serve

1 Toss the chicken in the sherry, and season with a little pepper.

2 Thread the chicken, mango, and bay leaves alternately on to long metal or presoaked wooden skewers, then brush lightly with oil.

3 Broil the skewers under a preheated medium-hot broiler for about 8–10 minutes, turning occasionally, until golden.

4 Sprinkle the skewers with the coconut and broil for another 30 seconds. Serve with salad greens.

NUTRITION

Calories 225; Sugars 11 g; Protein 31 g; Carbohydrate 11 g; Fat 6 g; Saturates 2 g

easy

20 mins

10 mins

🍳 **COOK'S TIP**

Use mangoes that are ripe but still firm so that they hold together on the skewers during cooking. Pineapple would also be suitable.

Chicken drumsticks are marinated to impart a tangy, sweet-and-sour flavor and a shiny glaze. Make sure they are cooked through thoroughly.

Sweet *and* Sour Drumsticks

1 Skin the chicken, if desired, and slash 2–3 times with a sharp knife.

2 Lay the chicken drumsticks side by side in a shallow, nonmetallic container.

3 Mix the red wine vinegar, tomato paste, soy sauce, honey, Worcestershire sauce, garlic, and cayenne pepper together and pour the mixture over the chicken drumsticks.

4 Leave to marinate in the refrigerator for 1 hour. Cook the drumsticks under a preheated medium-hot broiler for about 20 minutes, brushing with the marinade and turning during cooking. Garnish with parsley and serve with a crisp salad.

SERVES 4

8 chicken drumsticks
4 tbsp red wine vinegar
2 tbsp tomato paste
2 tbsp soy sauce
2 tbsp honey
1 tbsp Worcestershire sauce
1 garlic clove
good pinch of cayenne pepper
sprigs of fresh parsley, to garnish
crisp salad, to serve

NUTRITION
Calories *171*; Sugars *9 g*; Protein *23 g*; Carbohydrate *10 g*; Fat *5 g*; Saturates *1 g*

 very easy

 1 hr 15 mins

20 mins

COOK'S TIP

For a tangy flavor, add the juice of 1 lime to the marinade. While the drumsticks are broiling, check regularly to ensure that they are not burning.

Warm weather calls for lighter eating, and this chilled chicken dish in a subtle herb vinaigrette is ideal for a summer dinner party or picnic.

Chicken *with* Garden Herbs

S E R V E S 4

4 skinless, part-boned chicken breasts
6 tbsp olive oil
2 tbsp lemon juice
4 tbsp finely chopped fresh summer herbs,
    such as parsley, chives, and mint
1 ripe avocado, pitted
½ cup lowfat fromage blanc
pepper

to serve
cold rice
fresh red chiles, slices
scallions, sliced

N U T R I T I O N
Calories 370; Sugars 3 g; Protein 33 g;
Carbohydrate 3 g; Fat 25 g; Saturates 04 g

easy

1 hr 15 mins

25 mins

1 Using a sharp knife, cut 3–4 deep slashes in the chicken breasts.

2 Place in a flameproof dish and brush lightly with a little of the oil.

3 Cook the chicken under a preheated medium-hot broiler, turning once, until golden and the juices run clear, not pink, when the meat is pierced in the thickest part with a skewer.

4 Combine the remaining oil with the lemon juice and herbs, and season with pepper to taste. Spoon the oil over the chicken and let cool. Chill in the refrigerator for at least 1 hour.

5 Mash the avocado or purée in a food processor with the fromage blanc. Season with pepper. Serve the chicken with the avocado sauce and rice, sprinkled with red chiles and scallions.

C O O K ' S   T I P

To remove the pit easily from an avocado, first cut it in half. Holding one half securely in your hand, rap the knife into the pit so that it becomes embedded in the pit, then carefully twist the knife to dislodge the pit.

These lowfat, spicy skewers are cooked in a matter of minutes. They can be assembled ahead of time and stored in the refrigerator until needed.

Skewered Spicy Tomato Chicken

1 Place the chicken in a bowl. Mix together the tomato paste, honey, Worcestershire sauce, and rosemary. Add to the chicken, stirring to coat it evenly.

2 Thread the chicken pieces and tomatoes alternately on to 8 presoaked wooden skewers.

3 Spoon any remaining glaze over. Cook under a preheated hot broiler for 8–10 minutes, turning occasionally, until the chicken is done. Garnish with sprigs of rosemary and serve on a bed of couscous.

SERVES 4

1 lb 2 oz/500 g skinless, boneless chicken breasts, cut into 1-inch/2.5-cm cubes
3 tbsp tomato paste
2 tbsp honey
2 tbsp Worcestershire sauce
1 tbsp chopped fresh rosemary
9 oz/250 g cherry tomatoes
sprigs of fresh rosemary, to garnish
couscous or rice, to serve

NUTRITION
Calories *195*; Sugars *11 g*; Protein *28 g*; Carbohydrate *12 g*; Fat *4 g*; Saturates *1 g*

 very easy

10 mins

10 mins

🍳 COOK'S TIP

Cherry tomatoes are ideal for barbecue grills as they can be threaded straight on to skewers. As they are kept whole, the skins retain the natural juices.

This Italian-style dish is richly flavored with pesto, which is a mixture of basil, olive oil, pine nuts, and Parmesan cheese. Red or green pesto can be used for this recipe.

Broiled Chicken *with* Pesto Toasts

SERVES 4

8 part-boned chicken thighs
olive oil, for brushing
1²∕₃ cups sieved tomatoes
½ cup green or red pesto sauce
12 slices French bread
1 cup grated Parmesan cheese
½ cup pine nuts or slivered almonds
salad greens, to serve

1 Arrange the chicken in a single layer in a wide, flameproof dish and brush lightly with oil.

2 Cook the chicken under a preheated broiler for about 15 minutes, turning occasionally, until golden brown and the juices run clear, not pink, when the meat is pierced in the thickest part with a skewer.

3 Pour off any excess fat. Warm the sieved tomatoes and half of the pesto sauce in a small pan and spoon it over the chicken. Broil for a few more minutes, turning until coated.

4 Meanwhile, spread the remaining pesto on to the bread and sprinkle with the Parmesan. Scatter the pine nuts over the cheese. Broil for 2–3 minutes, until browned and bubbling. Serve with a selection of salad greens.

NUTRITION
Calories 787; Sugars 6 g; Protein 45 g;
Carbohydrate 70 g; Fat 38 g; Saturates 9 g

easy
10 mins
25 mins

🍴 **COOK'S TIP**

Although leaving the skin on the chicken means that it will have a higher fat content, many people like its rich taste and crisp texture, especially when it is blackened by the broiler. The skin also seals in the cooking juices.

Great for barbecue grills, or for simple summer lunches and picnics, this is an easy and tasty chicken dish.

Mustard Barbecue Drummers

1 Chop 2 of the bacon slices into small pieces and dry-fry for 3–4 minutes, stirring so that the bacon does not stick to the bottom of the pan. Remove from the heat and stir in the garlic, 2 tablespoons of the whole-grain mustard, and the bread crumbs.

2 Carefully loosen the skin from each drumstick with your fingers, being careful not to tear the skin. Spoon a little of the mustard stuffing under each flap of skin, smoothing the skin over firmly afterward.

3 Wrap a bacon slice around each drumstick, and secure with toothpicks.

4 Mix together the remaining mustard and the oil, brush it over the chicken drumsticks, and cook on a preheated medium-hot barbecue grill or broiler for about 25 minutes, until the juices run clear, not pink, when the meat is pierced in the thickest part with a skewer.

5 Garnish with the parsley sprigs and serve hot or cold.

SERVES 4

10 smoked lean bacon slices
1 garlic clove, chopped finely
3 tbsp whole-grain mustard
4 tbsp fresh brown bread crumbs
8 chicken drumsticks
1 tbsp sunflower oil
sprigs of fresh parsley, to garnish

NUTRITION
Calories 394; Sugars 5 g; Protein 40 g; Carbohydrate 3 g; Fat 27 g; Saturates 8 g

 moderate

 20 mins

30 mins

🍳 COOK'S TIP

Don't cook the chicken over the hottest part of the barbecue grill or the outside may be charred before the center is cooked.

CHICKEN

These tangy lime and honey-coated pieces have a matching sauce, based on creamy plain yogurt. They could be served at a barbecue or as a main course for a dinner party.

Minty Lime Chicken

SERVES 6

3 tbsp finely chopped fresh mint
4 tbsp clear honey
4 tbsp lime juice
12 boneless chicken thighs

sauce
½ cup thick plain yogurt
1 tbsp finely chopped fresh mint
2 tsp finely grated lime zest
mixed salad, to serve

1 Combine the mint, honey, and lime juice in a shallow nonmetallic dish.

2 Use toothpicks to keep the chicken thighs in neat shapes and add the chicken to the marinade, turning to coat evenly.

3 Marinate for at least 30 minutes, preferably overnight. Cook the chicken on a preheated medium-hot broiler or over hot coals, turning frequently and basting with the marinade. The chicken is done if the juices run clear, not pink, when the meat is pierced in the thickest part with a skewer.

4 Meanwhile, mix together the sauce ingredients.

5 Remove the toothpicks and serve the chicken with a salad and the sauce.

NUTRITION
Calories *170*; Sugars *12 g*; Protein *23 g*;
Carbohydrate *12 g*; Fat *3 g*; Saturates *1 g*

 easy
40 mins
20 mins

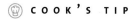 **COOK'S TIP**

Mint can be grown very easily in a garden or window box. It is a useful herb for marinades and salad dressings. Other useful herbs are parsley and basil.

This fall recipe can be made with fresh-picked wild blackberries from the hedgerow if you're lucky enough to have a good supply near you.

Chicken Kebabs *with* Blackberry Sauce

1 Place the chicken in a bowl. Sprinkle with the white wine and rosemary, and season with pepper to taste. Cover and marinate in the refrigerator for at least 1 hour.

2 Drain the chicken, reserving the marinade, and thread the meat onto 8 metal or presoaked wooden skewers.

3 Cook under a preheated medium-hot broiler for 8–10 minutes, turning, until golden and evenly cooked.

4 Meanwhile, to make the sauce, place the marinade in a pan with the blackberries and simmer gently until soft. Press the mixture though a strainer using the back of a spoon.

5 Return the blackberry sauce to the pan with the cider vinegar and red currant jelly and bring to a boil. Boil, uncovered, until the sauce has reduced by about one-third.

6 Place the chicken skewers on serving plates and drizzle with the bramble sauce. Sprinkle with nutmeg and serve hot, garnished with rosemary and blackberries, with a green salad.

COOK'S TIP

If you use canned fruit, omit the red currant jelly.

SERVES 4

4 skinless, boneless chicken breasts or
    8 thighs, cut into 1-inch/2.5-cm pieces
4 tbsp dry white wine or hard cider
2 tbsp chopped fresh rosemary
pepper
salad greens, to serve

to garnish
sprigs of fresh rosemary
blackberries

sauce
scant 2 cups blackberries
1 tbsp cider vinegar
2 tbsp red currant jelly
1/4 tsp grated nutmeg

NUTRITION
Calories 174; Sugars 5 g; Protein 27 g;
Carbohydrate 5 g; Fat 4 g; Saturates 1 g

easy

1 hr 15 mins

20 mins

Here, spatchcocked Squabs are complemented by the delicate fragrance of lemon and tarragon.

Tarragon Squabs *with* Lemon

SERVES 2

2 Squabs
4 sprigs of fresh tarragon
1 tsp oil
2 tbsp butter
zest of ½ lemon
1 tbsp lemon juice
1 garlic clove, crushed
salt and pepper
new potatoes, to serve

to garnish
sprigs of fresh tarragon
orange slices

1 Prepare the Squabs: turn them breast-side down on a cutting board and cut them through the backbone using kitchen scissors. Crush each bird gently to break the bones so that they lie flat while cooking. Season each with salt.

2 Turn them over and insert a sprig of tarragon under the skin over each side of the breast.

3 Brush the birds with oil, using a pastry brush, and place under a preheated hot broiler about 5-inches/13-cm from the heat. Broil for about 15 minutes, turning half way through, until they are lightly browned.

4 Meanwhile, to make the glaze, melt the butter in a small pan, add the lemon zest and juice, and garlic, and season with salt and pepper to taste.

5 Brush the Squabs with the glaze and cook for another 15 minutes, turning them once and brushing regularly so that they stay moist. Garnish with tarragon and orange slices, and serve with new potatoes.

NUTRITION
Calories *449*; Sugars *2 g*; Protein *38 g*; Carbohydrate *5 g*; Fat *30 g*; Saturates *10 g*

moderate

20 mins

35 mins

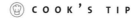 **COOK'S TIP**

Once the chickens are flattened, insert 2 metal skewers through them to keep them in place.

Chicken quarters are grilled, then served with aïoli, a strongly flavored garlic mayonnaise, which originated in Provence in the South of France.

Chicken *with* Warm Aïoli

1 Using a skewer, prick the chicken quarters in several places and place them in a shallow dish.

2 Combine the oil, lemon juice, and thyme, and season with salt and pepper to taste. Pour the mixture over the chicken, turning to coat the chicken evenly. Set aside in the refrigerator for 2 hours.

3 To make the aïoli, beat together the garlic and a pinch of salt to make a paste. Add the egg yolks and beat well. Gradually add the oils, drop by drop, beating vigorously, until the mayonnaise becomes creamy and smooth. Stir in the lemon juice and season with pepper. Set aside in a warm place.

4 Place the chicken over preheated coals and cook for 25–30 minutes. Brush with the marinade and turn the portions to cook evenly. Remove and arrange on a serving plate.

5 Beat the water into the aïoli and spoon into a warm serving bowl. Serve the chicken with the aïoli, salad greens, and lemon slices.

SERVES 4

4 chicken quarters
2 tbsp oil
2 tbsp lemon juice
2 tsp dried thyme
salt and pepper
lemon slices, to garnish
salad greens, to serve

aïoli

5 garlic cloves, chopped finely
2 egg yolks
½ cup each olive oil and sunflower oil
2 tsp lemon juice
2 tbsp boiling water

NUTRITION
Calories *873*; Sugars *0 g*; Protein *40 g*; Carbohydrate *1 g*; Fat *79 g*; Saturates *12 g*

 moderate

2 hrs 35 mins

30 mins

🍴 **COOK'S TIP**

To make a quick aïoli, add the garlic to 1¼ cups good-quality mayonnaise, then place in a bowl over a pan of warm water and beat together. Beat in 1–2 tablespoons of hot water just before serving.

These unusual chicken kebabs have a wonderful Mediterranean flavor, and the bacon helps to keep them moist.

Skewered Chicken Spirals

SERVES 4

4 skinless, boneless chicken breasts
1 garlic clove, chopped finely
2 tbsp tomato paste
4 smoked bacon slices
large handful of fresh basil leaves
oil, for brushing
salt and pepper
salad greens, to serve

1 Spread out a piece of chicken between 2 sheets of plastic wrap and beat firmly with a rolling pin to flatten the chicken to an even thickness. Repeat with the remaining pieces of chicken.

2 Mix together the garlic and tomato paste until well blended. Spread the mixture evenly over the chicken.

3 Lay a bacon slice over each piece of chicken, then scatter with the fresh basil leaves. Season with salt and pepper to taste.

4 Roll up each piece of chicken firmly, then cut into thick slices using a sharp knife. Thread the slices securely on to 4 pre-soaked wooden skewers, making sure the skewer holds the chicken in a spiral shape.

5 Brush the skewers lightly with oil and cook on preheated hot coals or broil for about 5 minutes, turn the skewers over, and cook for another 5 minutes, until the chicken is done. Serve the chicken spirals hot with salad greens.

NUTRITION
Calories *231*; Sugars *1 g*; Protein *29 g*;
Carbohydrate *1 g*; Fat *13 g*; Saturates *5 g*

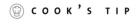

easy

15 mins

10 mins

 COOK'S TIP

Serve these kebabs with Parmesan-topped garlic bread.

Tomato catsup is a very popular ingredient in Asian dishes, as it imparts a zingy sweet-sour flavor.

Filipino Chicken

1 Combine the lemonade, gin, tomato catsup, garlic salt, and Worcestershire sauce in a large nonmetallic dish. Season with salt and pepper to taste.

2 Put the chicken into the dish and turn to coat them in the marinade.

3 To marinate in the refrigerator for 2 hours. Remove and let stand, covered at room temperature for 30 minutes.

4 Place the chicken over a medium-hot barbecue and grill for 20 minutes. Turn the chicken once, halfway through the cooking time.

5 Remove from the barbecue and let rest for 3–4 minutes before serving with egg noodles, tossed with a little green chile and scallions.

SERVES 4

1 can lemonade or lime-and-lemonade
2 tbsp gin
4 tbsp tomato catsup
2 tsp garlic salt
2 tsp Worcestershire sauce
4 skinless chicken suprêmes or breast fillets
salt and pepper

to serve
thread egg noodles
1 fresh green chile, chopped finely
2 scallions, sliced

NUTRITION
Calories *194*; Sugars *7 g*; Protein *28 g*; Carbohydrate *8 g*; Fat *4 g*; Saturates *1 g*

 easy

2 hrs 45 mins

20 mins

🍳 **COOK'S TIP**

Cooking the meat on the bone after it has reached room temperature means that it requires less time to cook, which ensures that the meat remains moist.

CHICKEN

These succulent chicken skewers are coated in a sweet lime dressing and are served with a lime and mango relish.

Lime Chicken Skewers

SERVES 4

4 skinless, boneless chicken breasts, about 4¹/₂ oz/125 g each, sliced thinly
3 tbsp lime marmalade
1 tsp white wine vinegar
¹/₂ tsp finely grated lime zest
1 tbsp lime juice
salt and pepper

to serve
lime wedges
white rice, sprinkled with chili powder

salsa
1 small mango, pitted and diced
1 small red onion, chopped finely
1 tbsp lime juice
1 tbsp chopped fresh cilantro

NUTRITION
Calories *199*; Sugars *14 g*; Protein *28 g*;
Carbohydrate *14 g*; Fat *4 g*; Saturates *1 g*

  easy

15 mins

10 mins

1 Thread the chicken on to 8 presoaked wooden skewers so that the meat forms an S-shape along each skewer.

2 Arrange the chicken skewers on a broiler rack. Combine the lime marmalade, vinegar, lime zest and juice. Season with salt and pepper to taste. Brush the marinade over the chicken and cook under a preheated broiler for 5 minutes. Turn the skewers over, brush with the marinade again, and broil for another 4–5 minutes.

3 Meanwhile, prepare the salsa. Mix together the mango, onion, lime juice, and fresh cilantro. Season to taste, cover, and chill until required.

4 Serve the chicken skewers with the salsa, accompanied with wedges of lime and plain rice.

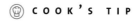 **COOK'S TIP**

To prevent sticking, lightly oil the metal skewers or dip wooden skewers in water before threading the chicken on to them.

Chicken tikka is a lowfat Indian dish. Recipes vary, and it is best to try your own combination of spices to suit your personal taste.

Chicken Tikka Kebabs

1 Place the chicken in a shallow, nonmetallic dish.

2 Combine the garlic, ginger, chile, yogurt, tomato paste, and spices, and season with salt and pepper to taste. Spoon the mixture over the chicken, cover, and chill for 2 hours.

3 Toss the mango in the lime juice, cover, and chill until required.

4 Thread the chicken and mango alternately on to 8 metal or presoaked wooden skewers. Place the skewers on a broiler rack and brush the chicken with the yogurt marinade and the lime juice left from the mango.

5 Place under a preheated medium-hot broiler for 6–7 minutes. Turn over, brush again with the marinade and lime juice, and cook for another 6–7 minutes, until the juices run clear, not pink, when the chicken is pierced in the thickest part with a skewer.

6 Serve the kebabs immediately on a bed of rice on a warm platter, garnished with fresh cilantro leaves and accompanied by lime wedges, salad greens, and nan bread.

SERVES **4**

4 skinless, boneless chicken breasts, about 4½ oz/125 g each, cut into 1-inch/ 2.5-cm cubes
1 garlic clove, crushed
1 tsp grated fresh gingerroot
1 fresh green chile, seeded and chopped finely
6 tbsp lowfat plain yogurt
1 tbsp tomato paste
1 tsp ground cumin
1 tsp ground coriander
1 tsp ground turmeric
1 large ripe mango, pitted and cubed
1 tbsp lime juice
salt and pepper
sprigs of fresh cilantro, to garnish

to serve
plain white rice
lime wedges
mixed salad greens
warm nan bread

NUTRITION
Calories *191*; Sugars *8 g*; Protein *30 g*; Carbohydrate *8 g*; Fat *4 g*; Saturates *2 g*

 easy

2 hrs 15 mins

15 mins

CHICKEN

You can use any chicken portions for this recipe. Thighs are economical for large barbecue parties, but you could also use wings or drumsticks.

Sweet Maple Chicken

SERVES 4

12 skinless, boneless chicken thighs
5 tbsp maple syrup
1 tbsp superfine sugar
grated zest and juice of $\frac{1}{2}$ orange
2 tbsp tomato catsup
2 tsp Worcestershire sauce

to garnish
orange slices
sprigs of fresh parsley

to serve
Italian bread, such as focaccia
salad greens
cherry tomatoes, quartered

1 Using a long sharp knife, make 2–3 diagonal slashes in the chicken to allow the flavors to permeate. Arrange the chicken thighs in a single layer in a shallow, nonmetallic dish.

2 To make the marinade, combine the maple syrup, sugar, orange zest and juice, tomato catsup, and Worcestershire sauce in a small bowl.

3 Pour the marinade over the chicken, turning the chicken to coat thoroughly. Cover with plastic wrap and chill in the refrigerator until required.

4 Remove the chicken from the marinade, reserving the marinade.

5 Transfer the chicken to the barbecue and broil over hot coals for 20 minutes, turning the chicken and basting frequently with the marinade. Alternatively, cook under a preheated medium-hot broiler for 20 minutes, turning and basting.

6 Transfer the chicken to warm serving plates and garnish with slices of orange and sprigs of parsley. Serve immediately with Italian bread, salad greens, and cherry tomatoes.

NUTRITION
Calories *122*; Sugars *16 g*; Protein *11 g*;
Carbohydrate *17 g*; Fat *1 g*; Saturates *1 g*

moderate

35 mins

20 mins

The chicken is marinated in an aromatic sauce before being cooked on the barbecue. Use bay leaves if kaffir lime leaves are unavailable.

Thai-style Chicken Skewers

1 To make the marinade, place the red curry paste in a small pan over medium heat and cook for 1 minute. Add half of the coconut milk to the pan and bring the mixture to a boil. Boil for 2–3 minutes, until the liquid has reduced by about two-thirds.

2 Remove the pan from the heat and stir in the remaining coconut milk. Set aside to cool.

3 Stir the chicken into the cold marinade, cover, and chill in the refrigerator for at least 2 hours.

4 Remove the chicken pieces from the marinade and thread them onto metal or pre-soaked wooden skewers, alternating the chicken with the vegetables and lime leaves.

5 Combine the oil and lime juice in a small bowl and brush the mixture over the kebabs. Grill the skewers over hot coals, turning and basting frequently, for 10–15 minutes, until the chicken is done. Grill the tomato halves for the last few minutes of the cooking time and serve with the chicken skewers.

SERVES 4

4 skinless, boneless chicken breasts, cut into 1-inch/2.5-cm pieces
1 onion, cut into wedges
1 large red bell pepper, seeded and cut into 1-cm/2.5-cm pieces
1 large yellow bell pepper, seeded and cut into 1-inch/2.5-cm pieces
12 kaffir lime leaves
2 tbsp sunflower oil
2 tbsp lime juice
tomato halves, to serve

marinade
1 tbsp Thai red curry paste
²⁄₃ cup canned coconut milk

NUTRITION
Calories *218*; Sugars *4 g*; Protein *28 g*; Carbohydrate *5 g*; Fat *10 g*; Saturates *2 g*

⭐⭐ easy
🕐 2 hrs 15 mins
🕐 20 mins

 COOK'S TIP

Cooking the marinade first intensifies the flavor. It is important to let the marinade cool before adding the chicken because any bacteria may breed in the warm temperature.

This is a barbecue variation of the traditional dish, Chicken Maryland. Serve with corn cobs.

Maryland Chicken Kebabs

SERVES 4

1 tbsp white wine vinegar
1 tbsp lemon juice
1 tbsp light corn syrup or honey
6 tbsp olive oil
1 garlic clove, crushed
8 skinless, boneless chicken thighs, cut into bite-size pieces
4 rindless smoked bacon slices
2 bananas, cut into 1-inch/2.5-cm pieces
salt and pepper

to serve
4 corn cobs
mango chutney

1 Combine the vinegar, lemon juice, syrup, oil, and garlic in a large bowl, stir well. Season with salt and pepper to taste. Add the chicken to the marinade and toss until coated. Cover and set aside in the refrigerator to marinate for 1–2 hours.

2 Stretch the bacon slices with the back of a knife, then cut each one in half. Brush the bananas with lemon juice to prevent them from turning brown. Wrap a piece of bacon around each piece of banana.

3 Remove the chicken from the marinade, reserving the marinade for basting. Thread the chicken pieces and the bacon and banana rolls alternately on to metal or presoaked wooden skewers.

4 Grill the kebabs over hot coals for 8–10 minutes, until the chicken is done. Baste them with the marinade and turn the skewers frequently.

5 Serve with corn cobs and mango chutney.

NUTRITION
Calories *443*; Sugars *14 g*; Protein *37 g*; Carbohydrate *16 g*; Fat *26 g*; Saturates *6 g*

 moderate
2 hrs 30 mins
10 mins

🅦 COOK'S TIP

For a quick Maryland-style dish, omit the marinating and cook the chicken thighs over hot coals for about 20 minutes, basting with the marinade. Broil the bananas in their skins beside the chicken.

Economical and flavorful, these tasty chicken liver skewers make an ideal light lunch or a perfect addition to a summer brunch party.

Sherried Liver Brochettes

1 To make the marinade, combine the sherry, oil, and mustard in a shallow dish. Season with salt and pepper to taste. Add the chicken livers to the marinade and toss until coated. Set aside to marinate for 3–4 hours.

2 To make the mayonnaise, stir the mustard into the mayonnaise and chill in the refrigerator.

3 Stretch the bacon with the back of a knife and cut each strip in half. Remove the chicken livers from the marinade, reserving the marinade for basting. Wrap the bacon around half of the chicken liver pieces. Thread the bacon and chicken liver rolls and the plain chicken liver pieces alternately on to 6 presoaked wooden skewers.

4 Broil the skewers over hot coals for about 10–12 minutes, turning and basting frequently with the reserved marinade.

5 Meanwhile, cut the bread into 6 pieces and toast the cut sides on the barbecue until golden brown.

6 To serve, top the toasted bread with the spinach leaves and place the brochettes on top. Spoon the mustard mayonnaise over and serve.

SERVES **4**

14 oz/400 g chicken livers, cut into 2-inch/5-cm pieces
3 rindless bacon slices
1 ciabatta loaf or small French stick
8 oz/225 g baby spinach leaves
salt and pepper

marinade
²⁄₃ cup dry sherry
4 tbsp olive oil
1 tsp whole-grain mustard

mustard mayonnaise
8 tbsp mayonnaise
1 tsp whole-grain mustard

NUTRITION
Calories *767*; Sugars *3 g*; Protein *31 g*; Carbohydrate *51 g*; Fat *43 g*; Saturates *8 g*

moderate

4 hrs 30 mins

15 mins

Spicy Dishes

Since chicken is so popular throughout the world, there are countless spicy recipes from Asia, Mexico, the Caribbean, Spain, and Japan. Lime juice, peanut, coconut and chile add the authentic tastes of Thailand to Chile Coconut Chicken, while Kashmiri Chicken is a rich and spicy dish from Northern India with an aromatic sauce made from plain yogurt, tikka curry paste, cumin, ginger, chilli and almonds. From Spain comes Chicken and Chorizo with Shrimp—a mixture of chicken and shellfish, together with the famous spicy Spanish sausage, chorizo, slow-cooked in a sauce of garlic, tomatoes and white wine. Lemon and Apricot Chicken is a creative modern dish that is perfect for any special occasion. There is even a dish from Japan, Teppanyaki, a simple dish of fried chicken with bell peppers, scallions, and beansprouts, served with a mirin dipping sauce.

This tasty chicken dish combines warm spices and almonds and is spiked with star anise to produce an exotic mix of flavors.

Warm Spiced Chicken *with* Almonds

SERVES 4

2 tbsp butter
⅓ cup vegetable oil
4 skinless, boneless chicken breasts, cut into
   2-inch x 1-inch/5-cm x 2.5-cm pieces
1 onion, chopped roughly
1-inch/2.5-cm piece of fresh gingerroot
3 garlic cloves
¼ cup blanched almonds
1 large red bell pepper, seeded and roughly
   chopped
1 tbsp ground cumin
2 tsp ground coriander
1 tsp ground turmeric
pinch of cayenne pepper
½ tsp salt
⅔ cup water
3 star anise
2 tbsp lemon juice
pepper
slivered almonds, to garnish
rice, to serve

NUTRITION

Calories *421*; Sugars *5 g*; Protein *33 g*;
Carbohydrate *7 g*; Fat *30 g*; Saturates *6 g*

✪✪✪   moderate

        20 mins

        50 mins

1 Heat the butter and 1 tablespoon of the oil in a skillet. Add the chicken and cook for 5 minutes, until golden. Transfer the chicken to a plate and keep warm until required.

2 Combine the onion, ginger, garlic, almonds, red bell pepper, ground cumin, ground coriander, turmeric, cayenne pepper, and salt in a food processor or blender. Blend to form a smooth paste.

3 Heat the remaining oil in a large pan or deep skillet. Add the spice paste and sauté for 10–12 minutes.

4 Add the chicken, water, star anise, and lemon juice, and season with pepper to taste. Reduce the heat, cover and simmer gently for 25 minutes, or until the chicken is tender, stirring occasionally.

5 Transfer the chicken to a serving dish, sprinkle with the slivered almonds, and serve with individual rice molds.

Serve this fruity curry with mango chutney and nan bread. Mangoes or pears make a good substitute for the pineapple.

Chicken *and* Pineapple Curry

1 Heat the oil in a large skillet. Coat the chicken in the seasoned flour and cook for about 4 minutes, until browned all over. Transfer the chicken to a large, deep casserole and keep warm until required.

2 Sauté the shallots, garlic, apples, pineapple, and golden raisins in the pan juices over low heat.

3 Add the honey, chicken bouillon, Worcestershire sauce, and hot curry paste. Season with salt and pepper to taste.

4 Pour the sauce over the chicken and cover the casserole with a lid or cooking foil. Cook in the center of a preheated oven, 350°F/180°C, for about 2 hours. Stir in the sour cream and cook for another 15 minutes. Serve the curry, garnished with the orange slices, with rice.

SERVES 4 – 6

1 tbsp oil
2 lb chicken meat, chopped
4 tbsp all-purpose flour, seasoned
32 shallots, chopped roughly
4 garlic cloves, crushed with a little olive oil
3 tart apples, peeled, cored and diced
1 pineapple, peeled, cored, and diced
¾ cup golden raisins
1 tbsp honey
1¼ cups chicken bouillon
2 tbsp Worcestershire sauce
3 tbsp hot curry paste
⅔ cup sour cream
salt and pepper
orange slices, to garnish
rice, to serve

NUTRITION
Calories *666*; Sugars *57 g*; Protein *57 g*; Carbohydrate *72 g*; Fat *19 g*; Saturates *6 g*

 moderate
25 mins
2 hrs 30 mins

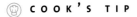 COOK'S TIP

Coconut rice also makes an excellent accompaniment to this dish.

Serve these easy-to-prepare tortillas to friends or as a quick supper. The chicken filling has a mild, mellow spicy heat and a fresh salad makes a perfect accompaniment.

Spicy Chicken Tortillas

SERVES 4

2 tbsp oil
8 skinless, boneless chicken thighs, sliced
1 onion, chopped
2 garlic cloves, chopped
1 tsp cumin seeds, crushed roughly
2 large dried chiles, sliced
14 oz/400 g canned tomatoes
14 oz/400 g canned red kidney beans,
    drained and rinsed
⅔ cup chicken bouillon
2 tsp sugar
salt and pepper
lime wedges, to garnish

to serve

1 large, ripe avocado, pitted
1 lime
8 soft tortillas
1 cup thick plain yogurt

1 Heat the oil in a preheated wok or large skillet. Add the chicken and sauté for 3 minutes, until golden. Add the onion and sauté for 5 minutes, stirring until browned. Add the garlic, cumin, and chiles, (with their seeds), and cook for about 1 minute.

2 Add the tomatoes, kidney beans, bouillon, and sugar, and season with salt and pepper to taste. Bring to a boil, breaking up the tomatoes. Reduce the heat, cover, and simmer for 15 minutes. Remove the lid and cook for 5 minutes, stirring occasionally, until the sauce has thickened.

3 Scoop out the avocado flesh on to a plate and mash with a fork. Cut half of the lime into 8 thin wedges. Squeeze the juice from the remaining lime over the avocado.

4 Warm the tortillas according to the instructions on the package. Put 2 tortillas on each serving plate, fill with the chicken mixture, and top with spoonfuls of avocado and yogurt. Garnish the tortillas with lime wedges.

NUTRITION

Calories *650*; Sugars *15 g*; Protein *48 g*;
Carbohydrate *47 g*; Fat *31 g*; Saturates *10 g*

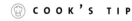 COOK'S TIP

For a vegetarian filling, replace the chicken with 14 oz/400 g canned pinto or cannellini beans, and use vegetable bouillon instead of the chicken bouillon.

 easy

 10 mins

 35 mins

This complete main course is cooked in one pan for simplicity. If you're cooking for one, simply halve the ingredients; the cooking time should stay the same.

Cajun Chicken Gumbo

1 Heat the oil in a wide pan and sauté the chicken until golden. Remove the chicken from the pan using a draining spoon. Stir in the onion, celery, and green bell pepper and sauté for 1 minute. Pour off any excess fat.

2 Add the rice and sauté, stirring briskly, for another 1 minute. Add the chicken bouillon and heat until boiling.

3 Add the chile and okra to the pan with the tomato paste. Season with salt and pepper to taste.

4 Return the chicken to the pan and stir. Cover tightly and simmer gently for 15 minutes, or until the rice is tender, the chicken is done and all the liquid has been absorbed. Stir occasionally and if the gumbo becomes too dry, add a little extra bouillon to moisten. Serve immediately.

SERVES 2

1 tbsp sunflower oil
4 chicken thighs
1 small onion, diced
2 celery stalks, diced
1 small green bell pepper, seeded and diced
½ cup long-grain rice
1¼ cups chicken bouillon
1 small red chile, sliced thinly
9 oz/250 g okra
1 tbsp tomato paste
salt and pepper

NUTRITION

Calories *425*; Sugars *8 g*; Protein *34 g*;
Carbohydrate *48 g*; Fat *12 g*; Saturates *3 g*

⭐⭐   easy

🕐   10 mins

🕐   25 mins

🧑‍🍳 COOK'S TIP

You can replace the chicken with 9 oz/250 g peeled shrimp and 3 oz/85 g belly of pork, if wished. Slice the pork and sauté in the oil before adding the onions, and add the shrimp 5 minutes before the end of the cooking time.

Easy to put together, this dish makes a perfect mid-week supper. Use tortilla chips instead of baking the tortillas, if preferred.

Green Chile *and* Chicken Chilaquiles

SERVES 4 – 6

12 stale tortillas, cut into strips
1 tbsp vegetable oil
1 small cooked chicken, meat removed from the bones and cut into bite-size pieces
Salsa Verde (see below)
3 tbsp chopped fresh cilantro
1 tsp finely chopped fresh oregano or thyme
4 garlic cloves, finely chopped
¼ tsp ground cumin
12 oz/350 g cheese, such as Cheddar, manchego, or mozzarella, grated
2 cups chicken bouillon
about 1⅓ cups grated Parmesan cheese

salsa verde

14 oz/400g green tomatoes, chopped finely
1–2 fresh green chiles, seeded and chopped
1 green bell pepper, seeded and chopped
1 small onion, chopped
1 bunch fresh cilantro, chopped finely
½ tsp ground cumin

NUTRITION

Calories *682*; Sugars *1 g*; Protein *60 g*; Carbohydrate *26 g*; Fat *38 g*; Saturates *20 g*

easy

20 mins

1 hr

1 Place the tortilla strips in a roasting pan, toss with the oil and bake in a preheated oven, 375°F/190°C, for 30 minutes, until crisp and golden.

2 Arrange the chicken in a 9 x 13-inch/23 x 33-cm casserole, then sprinkle with half of the salsa verde, cilantro, oregano, garlic, ground cumin, and some of the soft cheese. Repeat these layers and top with the tortilla strips.

3 Pour the stock over the top, then sprinkle with the remaining cheese.

4 Bake in the oven for about 30 minutes, until heated through and the cheese is lightly golden.

5 Serve garnished with the crème fraîche, scallions and pickled chillies.

COOK'S TIP

For a vegetarian Mexican filling, add diced sautéed bean curd and corn kernels in place of the cooked chicken.

Roasted garlic and mixed spices lend an evocative aroma to this tangy dish of simmered chicken, a speciality of Valladolid in the Yucatán peninsula.

Chicken *with* Yucatán Sauce

1 Place the chicken in a pan with enough bouillon to cover. Bring to a boil, then reduce the heat and simmer for 5 minutes. Remove from the heat and let the chicken cool in the bouillon; it will continue to cook as it cools.

2 Meanwhile, roast the garlic cloves in an ungreased heavy-based, nonstick skillet until they are lightly browned on all sides and tender inside. Remove from the heat. When cool enough to handle, squeeze the flesh from the skins and place in a bowl.

3 Grind the garlic with the pepper, ground cloves, oregano, salt, lime juice, and three-quarters of the cumin seeds. Mix with the flour.

4 When the chicken is cool, remove from the bouillon and pat dry. Reserve the bouillon. Rub the chicken with about two-thirds of the garlic-spice paste and stand at room temperature for at least 30 minutes, or up to overnight in the refrigerator.

5 Fry the onions and chiles in a little of the oil until golden brown and softened. Pour in the vinegar and remaining cumin seeds, cook for a few minutes, then add the reserved bouillon and remaining spice paste. Boil, stirring, for about 10 minutes, until reduced in volume.

6 Dredge the chicken in flour. Heat the remaining oil in a heavy-based skillet. Fry the chicken until lightly browned, then remove from the pan and serve immediately, topped with the onion and vinegar sauce.

SERVES 4 – 6

8 small boned chicken thighs
chicken bouillon
15–20 garlic cloves, unpeeled
1 tsp coarsely ground black pepper
1/2 tsp ground cloves
2 tsp crumbled dried oregano or 1/2 tsp crushed or powdered bay leaves
about 1/2 tsp salt
1 tbsp lime juice
1 tsp cumin seeds, toasted lightly
1 tbsp flour, plus extra for dredging the chicken
3–4 onions, sliced thinly
2 fresh chiles, preferably mildish yellow ones, such as Mexican Guero or similar Turkish or Greek chiles, seeded and sliced
1 cup vegetable oil
scant 1/2 cup hard cider or sherry vinegar

NUTRITION

Calories *313*; Sugars *6 g*; Protein *15 g*; Carbohydrate *14 g*; Fat *22 g*; Saturates *3 g*

⭐⭐⭐   moderate

🕐   1 hr

🕐   25 mins

Chile, tomatoes, and corn are typical ingredients in a Mexican dish.

Mexican Drumsticks

SERVES 4

2 tbsp oil
8 chicken drumsticks
1 onion, chopped finely
1 tsp chili powder
1 tsp ground coriander
14 oz/400 g canned chopped tomatoes
2 tbsp tomato paste
⅔ cup frozen corn
salt and pepper
rice and mixed bell pepper salad, to serve

1 Heat the oil in a large skillet. Add the chicken drumsticks and cook over a medium heat until lightly browned. Remove the chicken drumsticks from the pan with a draining spoon and set aside until required.

2 Add the onion to the pan and cook for 3–4 minutes, until softened, then stir in the chili powder and ground coriander and cook for a few seconds, stirring briskly so the spices do not burn. Add the tomatoes and the tomato paste and stir well to combine.

3 Return the chicken drumsticks to the pan and simmer the casserole gently for 20 minutes, until the chicken is tender and thoroughly cooked. Add the corn and cook for another 3–4 minutes. Season with salt and pepper.

4 Serve with a rice and mixed bell pepper salad.

NUTRITION
Calories *207*; Sugars *8 g*; Protein *18 g*;
Carbohydrate *13 g*; Fat *9 g*; Saturates *2 g*

easy
5 mins
35 mins

 COOK'S TIP

Mexican dishes are not usually suitable for freezing because the strong flavors they contain, such as chile, intensify during freezing, and if left for too long can result in an an unpleasant, musty taste.

This tasty chicken stir-fry is quick and easy to make and is full of fresh flavors and crunchy vegetables.

Chicken *with* Black Bean Sauce

1 Put the chicken in a bowl. Add a pinch of salt and the cornstarch, and cover with water. Leave for 30 minutes.

2 Heat 1 tablespoon of the oil in a preheated wok or large, heavy-based skillet and stir-fry the chicken for 4 minutes. Transfer the chicken to a warm serving dish and clean the wok.

3 Add the remaining oil to the wok and add the garlic, black bean sauce, green and red bell peppers, chile, mushrooms, onion, and scallions. Stir-fry the vegetables for 2 minutes, then return the chicken to the wok.

4 Add the seasoning, stir–fry for 3 minutes, and thicken with a little of the cornstarch paste. Serve with noodles.

SERVES 4

14 oz/400 g chicken breasts, sliced thinly
pinch of cornstarch
2 tbsp oil
1 garlic clove, chopped finely
1 tbsp black bean sauce
1 each small red and green bell pepper, seeded and cut into strips
1 fresh red chile, chopped finely
1 cup sliced white mushrooms
1 onion, chopped
6 scallions, chopped
salt and pepper
fresh noodles, to serve

seasoning
½ tsp salt
½ tsp sugar
3 tbsp chicken bouillon
1 tbsp dark soy sauce
2 tbsp beef bouillon
2 tbsp rice wine
1 tsp cornstarch, blended with a little rice wine

NUTRITION
Calories 205; Sugars 4 g; Protein 25 g; Carbohydrate 6 g; Fat 9 g; Saturates 2 g

 moderate

40 mins

10 mins

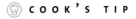 **COOK'S TIP**

Black bean sauce can be found in specialist shops and in many stores. Use dried noodles if you can't find fresh noodles.

This simple, Japanese-style cooking is ideal for thinly sliced chicken. Mirin is a rich, sweet rice wine which is available from Asian and other stores.

Teppanyaki

SERVES 4

1 red bell pepper, seeded and sliced thinly
1 green bell pepper, seeded and sliced thinly
4 scallions, sliced thinly
8 baby corn cobs, sliced thinly
½ cup bean sprouts
4 boneless chicken breasts, cut into ¼-inch/
   5-mm pieces
1 tbsp sesame or sunflower oil
4 tbsp soy sauce
4 tbsp mirin
1 tbsp grated fresh gingerroot

1 Arrange the bell peppers, scallions, corn, and bean sprouts on a plate with the chicken.

2 Heat a large griddle or heavy-based skillet, then lightly brush with oil. Add the vegetables and chicken in small batches, allowing space between them so they cook evenly and thoroughly.

3 In a small bowl, mix together the soy sauce, mirin, and ginger and serve as a dip with the chicken and vegetables.

NUTRITION
Calories 206; Sugars 4 g; Protein 30 g;
Carbohydrate 6 g; Fat 7 g; Saturates 2 g

  easy

 10 mins

10 mins

COOK'S TIP

Instead of serving the sauce as a dip, you could use it as a marinade. However, do not leave the chicken to marinate for more than 2 hours as the soy sauce will cause it to dry out and become tough.

This exotic dish can be made with any cut of chicken, but drumsticks are best for quick and even cooking. Grated fresh coconut adds a delicious, tropical flavor.

Caribbean Chicken

1 With a sharp knife, slash the chicken drumsticks at intervals, then place in a large bowl.

2 Sprinkle the lime juice over the chicken with the cayenne pepper. Cover and chill in the refrigerator for at least 2 hours or overnight.

3 Drain the chicken drumsticks using a draining spoon and reserve the juice. Heat the oil in a wide pan and sauté the chicken drumsticks, turning frequently, until golden. Stir in the marinade, lime rind, mango, and the dark brown sugar.

4 Cover the pan and simmer gently, stirring occasionally, for 15 minutes, or until the juices run clear when the chicken is pierced in the thickest part with a skewer. Garnish with coconut, lime wedges, and fresh cilantro.

SERVES 4

8 skinless chicken drumsticks
grated zest and juice of 2 limes
1 tsp cayenne pepper
2 mangoes, pitted and sliced
1 tbsp sunflower oil
2 tbsp dark brown sugar

to garnish

2 tbsp coarsely grated coconut
lime wedges
sprigs of fresh cilantro

NUTRITION

Calories *283*; Sugars *21 g*; Protein *24 g*; Carbohydrate *21 g*; Fat *12 g*; Saturates *3 g*

 easy

2 hrs 20 mins

30 mins

 COOK'S TIP

When buying mangoes, bear in mind that the skin of ripe mangoes varies in color from green to pinky-red and the flesh from pale yellow to bright orange. Choose mangoes which yield to gentle pressure.

This unusual dish, with its mixture of chicken and shellfish, is typically Spanish. The basis of this recipe is *sofrito*: a slow-cooked mixture of onion and tomato in olive oil, with garlic and peppers.

Chicken *and* Chorizo *with* Shrimp

SERVES 4

1 tbsp olive oil
4 skinless chicken quarters
1 red bell pepper, seeded and sliced
1 onion, sliced
2 garlic cloves, crushed
14 oz/400 g canned chopped tomatoes
scant 1 cup dry white wine
4 tbsp chopped fresh oregano
1 cup chorizo sausage, thinly sliced
1 cup peeled cooked shrimp
salt and pepper
rice, to serve

1 Heat the oil in a wide pan and sauté the chicken, turning occasionally, until golden brown.

2 Add the red bell pepper and onion to the pan and sauté until softened.

3 Add the garlic with the tomatoes, wine, and oregano. Season with salt and pepper to taste, then bring to a boil. Reduce the heat, cover and simmer gently for 45 minutes, or until the chicken is tender and the juices run clear, not pink, when the chicken is pierced in the thickest part with a skewer.

4 Add the chorizo to the pan with the shrimp, then simmer for another 5 minutes. Adjust the seasoning to taste and serve with rice.

NUTRITION
Calories *470*; Sugars *9 g*; Protein *52 g*;
Carbohydrate *10 g*; Fat *21 g*; Saturates *6 g*

easy

20 mins

1 hr

(☺) **COOK'S TIP**

Chorizo is a spicy Spanish sausage made with pork and a hot pepper such as cayenne or pimento. It is available from large stores and specialist butchers.

For this very popular dish, small pieces of chicken are marinated in a creamy mixture of plain yogurt and spices

Chicken Tikka

1 Blend together the ginger, garlic, ground coriander, ground cumin, and chili powder in a large mixing bowl.

2 Add the yogurt, salt, lemon juice, red food coloring (if using), and the tomato paste to the spice mixture.

3 Add the chicken to the spice mixture and toss to coat well. Marinate in the refrigerator for at least 3 hours, preferably overnight.

4 Arrange the onion in the bottom of a heatproof dish. Carefully drizzle half of the oil over the onions.

5 Arrange the marinated chicken pieces on top of the onions and cook under a preheated medium-hot broiler, turning once and basting with the remaining oil, for 25–30 minutes.

6 Serve on a bed of lettuce and garnish with the lemon wedges.

SERVES 6

1 tsp finely chopped fresh gingerroot
1 tsp fresh garlic, chopped finely
½ tsp ground coriander
½ tsp ground cumin
1 tsp chili powder
3 tbsp yogurt
1 tsp salt
2 tbsp lemon juice
few drops of red food coloring (optional)
1 tbsp tomato paste
3 lb 5 oz/1.5 kg chicken breasts, cut into bite-size pieces
1 onion, sliced
3 tbsp oil
6 lettuce leaves
1 lemon, cut into wedges, to garnish

NUTRITION

Calories *173*; Sugars *6 g*; Protein *28 g*; Carbohydrate *6 g*; Fat *4 g*; Saturates *2 g*

  easy

3 hrs 20 mins

  30 mins

🍴 **COOK'S TIP**

Chicken Tikka can be served with nan bread, relish, and raita, which is a mixture of chopped garlic, cucumber, and plain yogurt.

This is a quick and tasty way to use leftover roast chicken. The sauce can also be used for other types of cooked meat, such as poultry, lamb or beef.

Chicken Jalfrezi

SERVES 4

1 tsp mustard oil
3 tbsp vegetable oil
1 large onion, chopped finely
3 garlic cloves, crushed
1 tbsp tomato paste
2 tomatoes, peeled and chopped
1 tsp ground turmeric
½ tsp ground cumin
½ tsp ground coriander
½ tsp chili powder
½ tsp garam masala
1 tsp red wine vinegar
1 small red bell pepper, seeded and chopped
1 cup frozen fava beans
1 lb/500 g cooked chicken breasts, cut into bite-size pieces
salt
sprigs of fresh cilantro, to garnish

NUTRITION
Calories 270; Sugars 3 g; Protein 36 g;
Carbohydrate 7 g; Fat 11 g; Saturates 2 g

easy
20 mins
20 mins

1 Heat the mustard oil in a large skillet set over high heat for about 1 minute, until it begins to smoke. Add the vegetable oil, reduce the heat, and add the onion and garlic. Sauté until golden.

2 Add the tomato paste, tomatoes, ground turmeric, ground cumin, ground coriander, chili powder, garam masala, and red wine vinegar to the skillet, then stir well.

3 Add the red bell pepper and fava beans and stir for 2 minutes, until the bell pepper has softened. Stir in the chicken, and season with salt to taste. Let simmer for 6–8 minutes, until the chicken is heated through and the beans are tender.

4 Serve garnished with cilantro sprigs.

COOK'S TIP

This dish is an ideal way of using up leftover poultry—turkey, duck, or quail. Any variety of beans works well, but vegetables are just as good, especially root vegetables, zucchini, potatoes, or broccoli.

This biryani recipe may look rather complicated, but is not difficult to follow. You can substitute lamb for the chicken.

Chicken Biryani

1 Blend together the ginger, garlic, garam masala, chili powder, turmeric, 1 teaspoon of the salt, and cardamom seeds, and mix with the yogurt and chicken pieces. Set aside to marinate for 3 hours.

2 Pour the milk into a pan and bring to a boil. Pour it over the saffron and set aside.

3 Heat the ghee in a pan and cook the onions until golden brown. Set aside.

4 Place the rice, cinnamon sticks, peppercorns, and black cumin seeds in a pan of water. Bring the rice to a boil and remove from the heat when half-cooked. Drain and place in a bowl. Mix with the remaining salt.

5 Add the chicken mixture to the pan with the onions and ghee. Add the chiles, cilantro, lemon juice, and saffron. Add the rice and the rest of the ingredients, and cover tightly. Cook over low heat for 1 hour. Check that the meat is done before serving. If the meat is not done, return it to the heat, and cook for another 15 minutes. Mix thoroughly before serving hot.

SERVES 4

1½ tsp finely chopped fresh gingerroot
1½ tsp crushed garlic
1 tbsp garam masala
1 tsp chili powder
½ tsp ground turmeric
2 tsp salt
20 green/white cardamom seeds, crushed
1¼ cups plain yogurt
3 lb 5 oz/1.5 kg skinless chicken, cut into 8 pieces
⅔ cup milk
saffron strands
6 tbsp ghee
2 onions, sliced
2¼ cups basmati rice, rinsed
2 cinnamon sticks
4 black peppercorns
1 tsp black cumin seeds
4 fresh green chiles, chopped finely
few fresh cilantro leaves, chopped finely
4 tbsp lemon juice

NUTRITION
Calories 382; Sugars 8 g; Protein 42 g;
Carbohydrate 10 g; Fat 20 g; Saturates 11 g

  moderate

3 hrs 20 mins

1 hr 30 mins

In India, tandoori chicken is traditionally cooked in a clay oven. Alternatively, a broiler produces a similarly delicious result.

Tandoori-style Chicken

SERVES 4

8 skinless chicken drumsticks
²/₃ cup plain yogurt
1½ tsp finely chopped fresh gingerroot
1½ tsp finely chopped fresh garlic
1 tsp chili powder
2 tsp ground cumin
2 tsp ground coriander
1 tsp salt
½ tsp red food coloring
1 tbsp tamarind paste
²/₃ cup water
²/₃ cup oil
lemon wedges, to garnish

to serve
lettuce leaves
onion rings
nan bread

1 Make 2–3 slashes in each piece of chicken.

2 Place the yogurt in a bowl. Add the ginger, garlic, chili powder, ground cumin, ground coriander, salt, and red food colouring and blend together until well combined.

3 Add the chicken to the yogurt and spice mixture and mix to coat well. Let the chicken marinate in the refrigerator for a minimum of 3 hours.

4 In a separate bowl, mix the tamarind paste with the water and fold into the yogurt and spice mixture. Toss the chicken pieces in this mixture and set aside to marinate for another 3 hours.

5 Transfer the chicken to a heatproof dish and brush the chicken with oil. Cook the chicken under a preheated medium-hot broiler for 30–35 minutes, turning the chicken pieces occasionally and basting with the remaining oil.

6 Arrange the chicken on a bed of lettuce and serve with the onion and nan bread. Garnish with lemon wedges.

NUTRITION
Calories *514*; Sugars *5 g*; Protein *28 g*;
Carbohydrate *6 g*; Fat *43 g*; Saturates *6 g*

easy

6 hrs 30 mins

35 mins

🍳 COOK'S TIP

A cooling raita of chopped garlic, cucumber, and plain yogurt will complement this dish perfectly.

Korma is a typically mild and aromatic curry. If you want to reduce the fat in this recipe, use plain yogurt instead of the cream.

Chicken Korma *with* Cilantro

1 Place the ingredients for the korma paste into a blender or food processor and blend together to make a smooth paste.

2 Place the chicken in a bowl and spoon the korma paste over. Stir to coat the chicken completely with the paste. Cover and chill in the refrigerator for 3 hours to allow the flavors to permeate the chicken.

3 Simmer the meat in a large pan for 25 minutes, adding a little chicken bouillon if the mixture becomes too dry.

4 Add the heavy cream and garam masala to the pan and simmer for another 15 minutes. Let the korma stand for 10 minutes before serving. Serve with rice and garnish with fresh cilantro.

SERVES 6

1 lb 10 oz/750 g chicken meat, cut into cubes
1¼ cups heavy cream
½ tsp garam masala

korma paste

2 garlic cloves
1-inch/2.5-cm piece of fresh gingerroot, chopped coarsely
⅓ cup blanched almonds
6 tbsp chicken bouillon
1 tsp ground cardamon
4 cloves, crushed
1 tsp cinnamon
2 large onions, chopped
1 tsp coriander seeds
2 tsp ground cumin
pinch of cayenne
6 tbsp olive oil
salt and pepper
rice, to serve
sprigs of fresh cilantro, to garnish

NUTRITION
Calories *488*; Sugars *6 g*; Protein *21 g*;
Carbohydrate *9 g*; Fat *42 g*; Saturates *17 g*

moderate

3 hrs 40 mins

40 mins

 COOK'S TIP

To prepare your own garam masala, grind 1 teaspoon cardamon seeds with 2 teaspoons cloves, 2 tablespoons each cumin and coriander seeds, a cinnamon stick, 1 tablespoon black peppercorns and 1 dried red chili.

CHICKEN

This roast chicken is accompanied by a spicy stuffing, including rice, garlic, cashews, and ginger.

Roast Chicken *with* Cashew Nuts

SERVES 4

1 chicken, weighing about 3 lb 5 oz/1.5 kg
1 small onion, halved
2 tbsp butter, melted
1 tsp ground turmeric
1 tsp ground ginger
½ tsp cayenne
salt and pepper

stuffing

2 tbsp oil
1 onion, chopped finely
½ red bell pepper, seeded and chopped finely
2 garlic cloves, finely chopped
½ cup basmati rice, rinsed
1½ cups hot chicken bouillon
grated zest of ½ lemon
½ tsp ground turmeric
½ tsp ground ginger
½ tsp ground coriander
pinch of cayenne pepper
½ cup salted cashews

NUTRITION

Calories 587; Sugars 5 g; Protein 52 g;
Carbohydrate 35 g; Fat 26 g; Saturates 8 g

★★★   moderate

         30 mins

         2 hrs

1 To make the stuffing, heat the oil in a pan. Add the onion, red bell pepper, and garlic, and cook gently for 4–5 minutes. Add the rice and stir to coat in the oil. Add the bouillon and bring to a boil.

2 Reduce the heat, then simmer for 15 minutes, until all the liquid has been absorbed. Transfer to a bowl and add the remaining ingredients for the stuffing. Season with pepper to taste.

3 Place half of the stuffing in the neck end of the chicken with the onion and secure with a toothpick. Spoon the rest of the rice stuffing into a greased ovenproof dish and cover with foil.

4 Place the chicken in a roasting pan. Prick all over avoiding the stuffed area. Mix together the butter and spices, season, then brush the mixture over the chicken.

5 Roast in a preheated oven, 375°F/190°C, for 1 hour, basting from time to time. Place the dish of rice stuffing in the oven and continue to cook the chicken for 30 minutes. Remove the toothpick and garnish with fresh cilantro. Serve the chicken with the stuffing and garnish with cilantro.

The intense flavors of this dish are helped by the slow, gentle cooking. The meat should be almost falling off the bone.

Braised Garlic Chicken

1 Place the garlic, shallots, chiles, lemongrass, cilantro, and shrimp paste in a pestle and mortar and grind to an almost smooth paste. Stir in the cinnamon and tamarind paste.

2 Heat the oil in a large, heavy-based skillet or preheated wok. Add the chicken pieces, turning frequently, until they are golden brown on all sides. Remove them from the skillet with a draining spoon and keep hot. Tip away any excess fat.

3 Add the garlic paste to the skillet and cook over medium heat, stirring constantly, until lightly browned. Stir in the bouillon and return the chicken to the skillet, then bring to a boil.

4 Reduce the heat, cover and simmer, stirring occasionally, for 25–30 minutes, until the chicken is tender and thoroughly cooked. Stir in the fish sauce and peanut butter and simmer gently for another 10 minutes.

5 Season with salt and pepper to taste and sprinkle the toasted peanuts over the chicken. Serve immediately, with the stir-fried vegetables and noodles.

SERVES 4

4 garlic cloves, chopped
4 shallots, chopped
2 small fresh red chiles, seeded and chopped
1 lemongrass stalk, outer leaves removed and chopped finely
1 tbsp chopped fresh cilantro
1 tsp shrimp paste
$\frac{1}{2}$ tsp ground cinnamon
1 tbsp tamarind paste
2 tbsp vegetable oil
8 chicken pieces, such as drumsticks or thighs
1$\frac{1}{4}$ cups chicken bouillon
1 tbsp Thai fish sauce
1 tbsp smooth peanut butter
4 tbsp chopped toasted peanuts
salt and pepper
stir-fried vegetables and noodles, to serve

NUTRITION
Calories *282*; Sugars *3 g*; Protein *29 g*;
Carbohydrate *5 g*; Fat *16 g*; Saturates *3 g*

✪✪✪   moderate
         15 mins
     1 hr

Coconut adds a creamy texture and delicious flavor to this Thai-style stir-fry, which is spiked with fresh green chile.

Chile Coconut Chicken

SERVES 4

3 tbsp sesame oil
12 oz/350 g chicken breasts, sliced thinly
8 shallots, sliced
2 garlic cloves, finely chopped
1-inch/2.5-cm piece of fresh gingerroot, grated
1 fresh green chile, chopped finely
1 each red and green bell pepper, seeded and sliced thinly
3 zucchini, sliced thinly
2 tbsp ground almonds
1 tsp ground cinnamon
1 tbsp oyster sauce
¼ cup creamed coconut, grated
salt and pepper

1 Heat the sesame oil in a preheated wok or large, heavy-based skillet. Add the chicken, season with salt and pepper to taste, and stir-fry for about 4 minutes.

2 Add the shallots, garlic, ginger, and chile and stir-fry for 2 minutes.

3 Add the red and green bell peppers and zucchini and cook for about 1 minute.

4 Add the remaining ingredients, then adjust the seasoning and stir-fry for 1 minute and serve.

NUTRITION
Calories *184*; Sugars *6 g*; Protein *24 g*;
Carbohydrate *8 g*; Fat *5 g*; Saturates *2 g*

 easy
15 mins
10 mins

 **COOK'S TIP**

Creamed coconut is sold in blocks. It is a useful pantry standby as it adds richness and depth of flavor to cooking.

These simple marinated chicken portions are packed with powerful, zesty flavors, best accompanied by plain rice and a cucumber salad.

Spicy Cilantro Chicken

1 Using a sharp knife, cut 3 deep slashes down the side of each chicken breast. Place the chicken in a single layer in a wide, nonmetallic dish.

2 Put the garlic, chile, ginger, cilantro, lime zest and juice, soy sauce, superfine sugar, and coconut milk in a food processor and process to a smooth paste.

3 Spread the paste over both sides of the chicken portions, coating them evenly. Cover the dish with plastic wrap and set aside to marinate in the refrigerator for about 1 hour.

4 Lift the chicken from the marinade, drain off the excess, and place in a broiler pan. Cook under a preheated broiler for 12–15 minutes, until thoroughly and evenly cooked.

5 Meanwhile, place the remaining marinade in a pan and bring to a boil. Reduce the heat and simmer for several minutes to heat thoroughly. Remove the pan from the heat.

6 Place the chicken breasts on warm serving plates and pour the sauce over. Serve immediately accompanied with plain rice and cucumber and radish salad.

SERVES 4

4 skinless, boneless chicken breasts
2 garlic cloves, peeled
1 fresh green chile, seeded
3/4-inch/2-cm piece of fresh gingerroot
4 tbsp chopped fresh cilantro
finely grated zest of 1 lime
3 tbsp lime juice
2 tbsp light soy sauce
1 tbsp superfine sugar
3/4 cup coconut milk

to serve
plain boiled rice
cucumber and radish salad

NUTRITION
Calories *171*; Sugars *8 g*; Protein *31 g*;
Carbohydrate *9 g*; Fat *2 g*; Saturates *0.5 g*

✪✪✪ moderate

1 hr 25 mins

20 mins

This quick dish has many variations, but this version includes the classic combination of peanuts, chicken, and chiles, blending together to give a wonderfully flavored dish.

Chile *and* Peanut Chicken

SERVES 4

2 tbsp peanut oil
1 cup shelled peanuts
10½ oz/300 g skinless, boneless chicken breasts, cut into 1-inch/2.5-cm cubes
1 fresh red chile, sliced
1 green bell pepper, seeded and cut into strips
fried rice, to serve

sauce

⅔ cup chicken bouillon
1 tbsp Chinese rice wine or dry sherry
1 tbsp light soy sauce
1½ tsp light brown sugar
2 garlic cloves, chopped finely
1 tsp grated fresh gingerroot
1 tsp rice wine vinegar
1 tsp sesame oil

1 Heat the peanut oil in a preheated wok. Add the peanuts and stir-fry for 1 minute. Remove the peanuts with a draining spoon and set aside.

2 Add the chicken to the wok and cook for 1–2 minutes. Stir in the chile and green bell pepper and cook for 1 minute. Remove from the wok with a draining spoon and set aside.

3 Put half of the peanuts in a food processor and process until almost smooth. Alternatively, place them in a plastic bag and crush them with a rolling pin.

4 To make the sauce, add the chicken bouillon, Chinese rice wine, soy sauce, sugar, garlic, ginger, and rice wine vinegar to the wok.

5 Heat the sauce without boiling and stir in the peanuts, chicken, chile, and green bell pepper.

6 Sprinkle the sesame oil into the wok, stir and cook for 1 minute. Serve hot with fried rice.

NUTRITION

Calories *324*; Sugars *3 g*; Protein *25 g*; Carbohydrate *6 g*; Fat *24 g*; Saturates *5 g*

moderate

15 mins

10 mins

🍳 **COOK'S TIP**

If necessary, process the peanuts with a little of the bouillon in step 4 to make a softer paste.

This is a simple version of a creamy textured and mildly spiced Indian pilau. Although there are lots of ingredients, very little preparation is needed for this dish.

Indian Chicken *and* Golden Raisin

1 Heat the butter in a heavy-based pan and sauté the chicken with the onion for about 3 minutes.

2 Stir in the ground turmeric, ground cinnamon, and rice, and season with salt and pepper to taste, then sauté gently for 3 minutes.

3 Add the yogurt, golden raisins, and chicken bouillon and mix well, then bring to a boil. Reduce the heat, cover and simmer for 10 minutes, stirring occasionally, until the rice is tender and the bouillon has been absorbed. Add more bouillon if the mixture becomes too dry.

4 Stir in the tomato and cilantro. Sprinkle the pilau with the toasted coconut and garnish with cilantro sprigs.

SERVES 4

4 tbsp butter
8 skinless, boneless chicken thighs, cut into large pieces
1 onion, sliced
1 tsp ground turmeric
1 tsp ground cinnamon
1 cup long-grain rice, rinsed
1¾ cups plain yogurt
⅓ cup golden raisins
scant 1 cup chicken bouillon
1 tomato, chopped
2 tbsp chopped fresh cilantro or parsley
2 tbsp toasted coconut
salt and pepper
sprigs of fresh cilantro, to garnish

NUTRITION

Calories *581*; Sugars *22 g*; Protein *31 g*; Carbohydrate *73 g*; Fat *19 g*; Saturates *12 g*

⭐⭐ easy

🕐 10 mins

🕐 25 mins

 COOK'S TIP

Long-grain rice is the most widely available, although basmati, with its slender grains, has a more aromatic flavour. Rice, especially basmati, should be washed thoroughly under cold, running water before use.

CHICKEN

This warming, rich, and spicy dish is based on the traditional cooking style of Northern India, using chicken on the bone.

Spiced Chicken *with* Pilau Rice

SERVES 4

4 skinless chicken drumsticks
4 skinless chicken thighs
⅔ cup plain yogurt
4 tbsp tikka curry paste
2 tbsp sunflower oil
1 onion, sliced thinly
1 garlic clove, crushed
1 tsp ground cumin
1 tsp finely chopped fresh gingerroot
½ tsp chili paste
4 tsp chicken bouillon
2 tbsp ground almonds
salt
fresh cilantro, to garnish

to serve
pilau rice
pickles
poppadums

NUTRITION
Calories *276*; Sugars *6 g*; Protein *28 g*;
Carbohydrate *8 g*; Fat *15 g*; Saturates *3 g*

moderate
1 hr 15 mins
35 mins

1 Using a sharp knife, slash the chicken fairly deeply at intervals and place in a large bowl.

2 Mix together the yogurt and curry paste and stir into the chicken, tossing to coat evenly. Cover and chill for at least 1 hour.

3 Heat the oil in a large pan. Sauté the onion and garlic for 4–5 minutes, until softened but not browned.

4 Stir in the ground cumin, ginger, and chili paste and cook gently for 1 minute.

5 Add the chicken and cook gently, turning from time to time, for about 10 minutes, or until evenly browned. Stir in any remaining marinade with the bouillon and almonds.

6 Cover the pan and simmer gently for another 15 minutes, or until the chicken is completely cooked and tender.

7 Season with salt to taste. Garnish the chicken with cilantro and serve with pilau rice, pickles, and poppadums.

COOK'S TIP

If preferred, use boneless chicken breasts instead of legs, and cut into large chunks for cooking.

Spiced chicken legs are partially boned and packed with dried apricots for an intense fruity flavor. A golden, spiced, lowfat yogurt coating keeps the chicken moist and tender.

Lemon *and* Apricot Chicken

1 Use a small sharp knife carefully to cut the flesh away from the thigh bone. Scrape the meat away down as far as the knuckle. Grasp the thigh bone firmly and twist it to break it away from the drumstick.

2 Open out the boned part of the chicken and sprinkle with the lemon zest, and season with pepper to taste. Pack the dried apricots into each piece of chicken. Fold over to enclose and secure with toothpicks.

4 Mix together the ground cumin, ground turmeric, and yogurt, and season with salt and pepper. Brush the mixture over the chicken to coat evenly. Place the chicken in an ovenproof dish or roasting pan and bake in a preheated oven, 375°F/190°C, for about 35–40 minutes, until the juices run clear, not pink, when the chicken is pierced in the thickest part with a skewer.

5 Meanwhile, cook the rice in boiling, lightly salted water until just tender, then drain well. Stir the hazelnuts and sunflower seeds into the rice. Serve the chicken with the nutty rice, lemon wedges, and salad greens.

SERVES 4

4 large skinless chicken leg quarters
finely grated zest of 1 lemon
1 cup ready-to-eat dried apricots
1 tbsp ground cumin
1 tsp ground turmeric
½ cup lowfat plain yogurt
salt and pepper

to serve

1½ cups brown rice
2 tbsp slivered hazelnuts or almonds, toasted
2 tbsp sunflower seeds, toasted
lemon wedges
salad greens

NUTRITION
Calories *305*; Sugars *21 g*; Protein *15 g*;
Carbohydrate *45 g*; Fat *8 g*; Saturates *1 g*

 moderate

20 mins

40 mins

This dinner party dish should ideally be cooked and served from a karahi, but if you do not have one, a deep, heavy skillet will do.

Herbed Chicken *with* Vegetables

SERVES 4

8 chicken drumsticks
1½ tsp finely chopped fresh gingerroot
1½ tsp crushed fresh garlic
1 tsp salt
2 onions, chopped
½ large bunch of fresh cilantro leaves
4–6 fresh green chiles
2½ cups oil
4 firm tomatoes, cut into wedges
2 large green bell peppers, seeded and roughly chopped

1 Make 2–3 slashes in each piece of chicken. Rub the ginger, garlic, and salt over the chicken pieces and set aside.

2 Place half of the onions, cilantro, and green chiles in a mortar and pestle and grind to a paste. Rub the paste over the chicken pieces.

3 Heat the oil in a preheated karahi or large skillet over a high heat. Add the remaining onions and sauté until golden brown. Remove the onions from the pan with a draining spoon and set aside.

4 Reduce the heat to medium-hot and sauté the chicken, in batches of about 2 at a time, until done (about 5–7 minutes). Drain on paper towels and keep warm while you cook the remaining batches; set aside

5 Add the tomatoes and the green bell peppers to the pan and half-cook them until they have softened but still have bite.

6 Transfer the tomatoes and bell peppers to a serving plate and arrange the chicken on top. Garnish with the reserved onions.

NUTRITION
Calories *499*; Sugars *10 g*; Protein *33 g*;
Carbohydrate *12 g*; Fat *36 g*; Saturates *6 g*

 easy

20 mins

45 mins

This tasty Thai-style dish has a classic sauce of lime, peanut, coconut, and fresh chile. You'll find coconut cream in most stores or delicatessens.

Thai Coconut Chicken

1 Place the chicken bouillon in a measuring pitcher and crumble the creamed coconut into the bouillon, stirring to dissolve.

2 Heat the oil in a preheated wok or large, heavy-based skillet and cook the chicken, stirring, until golden.

3 Add the red chile and the scallions to the wok and cook gently for a few minutes, stirring until combined.

4 Add the peanut butter, coconut cream mixture, lime zest and juice, and simmer uncovered, stirring, for about 5 minutes.

5 Serve with plain rice, garnished with scallion flowers and red chiles.

SERVES 4

²/₃ cup hot chicken bouillon
¹/₃ cup coconut cream
1 tbsp sunflower oil
8 skinless, boneless chicken thighs, cut into long, thin strips
1 small fresh red chile, sliced thinly
4 scallions, sliced thinly
4 tbsp smooth or crunchy peanut butter
finely grated zest and juice of 1 lime
plain rice, to serve

to garnish
scallion "flowers"
fresh red chiles

NUTRITION
Calories *348*; Sugars *2 g*; Protein *36 g*;
Carbohydrate *3 g*; Fat *21 g*; Saturates *8 g*

 ✪✪   easy
         🕐   10 mins
         🕐   15 mins

🍳 **COOK'S TIP**

Limes are used frequently in Thai cooking, particularly in conjunction with sweet flavors, such as coconut.